SKILLFUL GRACE

RANGJUNG YESHE BOOKS • *www.rangjung.com*

PADMASAMBHAVA: *Treasures from Juniper Ridge* •
Advice from the Lotus-Born • *Dakini Teachings* •
Following in Your Footsteps: The Lotus-Born Guru in Nepal •
Following in Your Footsteps: The Lotus-Born Guru in India

PADMASAMBHAVA AND JAMGÖN KONGTRÜL:
The Light of Wisdom, Vol. 1, Vol. 2, Vol. 3, Secret, Vol. 4 & Vol. 5

PADMASAMBHAVA, CHOKGYUR LINGPA, JAMYANG KHYENTSE WANGPO,
TULKU URGYEN RINPOCHE, ORGYEN TOBGYAL RINPOCHE, & OTHERS
Dispeller of Obstacles • *The Tara Compendium* •
Powerful Transformation • *Dakini Activity*

YESHE TSOGYAL: *The Lotus-Born*

DAKPO TASHI NAMGYAL: *Clarifying the Natural State*

TSELE NATSOK RANGDRÖL: *Mirror of Mindfulness* • *Heart Lamp*

CHOKGYUR LINGPA: *Ocean of Amrita* • *The Great Gate* • *Skillful Grace* •
Great Accomplishment • *Guru Heart Practices*

TRAKTUNG DUDJOM LINGPA: *A Clear Mirror*

JAMGÖN MIPHAM RINPOCHE:
Gateway to Knowledge, Vol. 1, Vol. 2, Vol. 3, & Vol. 4

TULKU URGYEN RINPOCHE: *Blazing Splendor* • *Rainbow Painting* •
As It Is, Vol. 1 & Vol. 2 • *Vajra Speech* • *Repeating the Words of the
Buddha* • *Dzogchen Deity Practice* • *Vajra Heart Revisited*

ADEU RINPOCHE: *Freedom in Bondage*

KHENCHEN THRANGU RINPOCHE: *Crystal Clear*

CHÖKYI NYIMA RINPOCHE: *Bardo Guidebook* •
Collected Works of Chökyi Nyima Rinpoche, Vol. 1 & Vol. 2

TULKU THONDUP: *Enlightened Living*

ORGYEN TOBGYAL RINPOCHE: *Life & Teachings of Chokgyur Lingpa* •
Straight Talk • *Sublime Lady of Immortality*

DZIGAR KONGTRÜL RINPOCHE: *Uncommon Happiness*

TSOKNYI RINPOCHE: *Fearless Simplicity* • *Carefree Dignity*

MARCIA BINDER SCHMIDT: *Dzogchen Primer* • *Dzogchen Essentials* •
Quintessential Dzogchen • *Confessions of a Gypsy Yogini* •
Precious Songs of Awakening Compilation

ERIK PEMA KUNSANG: *Wellsprings of the Great Perfection* •
A Tibetan Buddhist Companion • *The Rangjung Yeshe Tibetan-
English Dictionary of Buddhist Culture & Perfect Clarity*

SKILLFUL GRACE

Tara Practice for Our Times

TEACHINGS BY TULKU URGYEN RINPOCHE &
TRULSHIK ADEU RINPOCHE

TRANSLATED AND EDITED BY MARCIA BINDER SCHMIDT
& ERIK PEMA KUNSANG

Rangjung Yeshe Publications
Flat 5a, Greenview Garden,
125 Robinson Road, Hong Kong

Address letters to:
Rangjung Yeshe Publications
Ka-Nying Shedrub Ling Monastery
P.O. Box 1200, Kathmandu, Nepal

www.rangjung.com
office@rangjung.com

1 3 5 7 9 8 6 4 2

First Paperback Edition 2007
Printed in the United States of America

Distributed to the book trade by:
Perseus Books/Publishers Group West

Publication data: isbn-10: 962-7341-61-4 (pbk.)
isbn-13: 978-962-7341-61-1 (pbk.)

Authors: Tulku Urgyen Rinpoche (1920-1996), Trulshik
Adeu Rinpoche.
Foreword by Tara Bennett-Goleman
Compiled and edited by Marcia Binder Schmidt. Translated
from the Tibetan by Erik Pema Kunsang (Erik Hein
Schmidt). Edited with Michael Tweed and Kerry Moran
First ed.
Title: Skillful Grace: Tara Teachings for Our Times
Tibetan title: legs so gsum gyi don khrid.
1. Vajrayana/Tara—tradition of pith instructions. 2.
Buddhism—Tibet. I. Title.

Cover art by Lhadripa Nawang Zangpo

Table of Contents

5

Join your palms and say:

Sublime and noble Lady with your circle,
Lovingly regard me with compassion, free of thought.
Bless me so the aims of all my prayers
Can be fulfilled without obstacles.

May the Buddha's teachings spread and flourish!
May its holders live in harmony and good health!
May obstacles that threaten them subside!
May their teachings and practice prosper!

May sickness and famine, fighting and strife, all recede!
May spiritual richness increase even further!
May the spiritual rulers' kingdoms expand!
May every country, near and far, have harmony!

Protect us from untimely death and the sixteen threats,
From menacing dreams and sinister omens,
From the miseries of samsara's lower realms,
From every peril, now and always!

Increase our life, merit, capacity, experience and
    realization!
May harmful notions not intrude!
May the twofold awakened mind arise, free of effort!
May our aims be fulfilled in accordance with the
    Dharma!

From now until supreme enlightenment,
Always guard us with your kindness
Like a mother protects her only child.
May we be indivisible from you!

Foreword

A few years back, we had the opportunity to receive teachings from the revered Adeu Rinpoche in Putoshan, China—the island of the compassionate deity Kuan Yin. We asked for teachings on the Noble Goddess Tara, the Tibetan equivalent of Kuan Yin. Having had this wish for many years, it seemed auspicious to receive the teachings on the compassionate wisdom of Tara while surrounded by shrines dedicated to her. Rinpoche generously offered the teachings on the entire path to enlightenment based on Tara, which are included in this book.

The inspiring guidance we received has had a profound impact on my life. Less than a year later, I was forced to deal with the tragic loss of my brother in a fatal auto accident. The truth of impermanence is never so direct and immediate as when we are forced to come to grips with the reality of life's insubstantial, impermanent nature.

These precious teachings on the compassionate wisdom of Tara turned out to be a profound refuge. Faced with such a devastating life experience, I reflected wholeheartedly on the empty, impermanent nature of this life, and felt disenchantment with ordinary pursuits.

I found myself coming back again and again to a line from Rinpoche's teachings: "The world and beings, mansion and deity, dissolve into luminous space." There was great solace in this insight into the impermanence of everything— the deity, my brother, my self, everyone and all things.

Embraced by the warmth of compassion, the solidity of self loses its grip. Gradually awakening from this trance of self-absorption is a reality that we can become more familiar with through practice. This is an important function of yidam practice or deity yoga.

As I came to see through Rinpoche's guidance, the deity represents the awakened state. Arya Tara inspires compassion and wisdom—the true nature of our mind. Through training, our ordinary perceptions are gradually transformed. We lighten up. Supported by the transparent nature of the deity, the habitual tendencies that obscure our authenticity become increasingly transparent. Through this new perception, we become brighter, more kind and compassionate, and more capable.

One of the special qualities attributed to this compassionate goddess is the capacity to help billions and billions of beings in whatever way they may need, manifesting in whatever form they will best relate. Such altruistic motivation is a force that Arya Tara inspires in us to help awaken our own compassionate urge to benefit others.

Once awakened, this intention itself makes it easier to be helpful. Intriguingly, one part of the brain that activates during compassion is in the area that controls motor activity, the very urge to act. This is another way the practice of Tara helps to bring more meaning into our lives. Our mind-stream gradually becomes more habituated to benefiting others, so that kindness and compassion increasingly become our preferred mode of choice.

As we awaken to the wisdom of our insubstantial nature, our sense of separateness dissolves. We realize how interdependent and interconnected all life is as we awaken to this wider perspective. As we touch the luminous wakefulness of our own true nature, we act more spontaneously for the wellbeing of others.

The guidance in this inspiring little book of Tara offers rare pearls of wisdom and jewels of compassion that can be integrated into our lives. As the late Nyoshul Khen Rinpoche, another of my teachers, once said about the teachings of the Dharma, "When you hold a jewel in your hand, don't let it go to waste." Life is precious.

—Tara Bennett-Goleman

PREFACE

The Essential Instruction on the Threefold Excellence contains three distinct views: Theravada, Mahayana and Vajrayana. The special approach it takes is to combine or interweave all three into a seamless single path that one person can follow. This small text begins in a simple way, with how to deal with life as a human being and goes all the way to how to attain true and complete enlightenment in a single lifetime.

The first level of the teachings here deals with being human. This means understanding that we have a precious opportunity right now in this life, and that it does matter how we behave: there are consequences to our actions. We are shown how to find the true spiritual path that leads us in the right direction.

The second level of teachings provides methods for reducing and dissolving our selfishness. It offers advice on how to genuinely work for others and gain mental stability and insight. In this teaching, insight is the core of Tara practice. Here it is called 'the ultimate Tara of transcendent knowledge.'

Once we have stability and insight—often called shamatha and vipashyana—we as practitioners can then embrace Vajrayana, the third level, with skillful means that quickly dissolve habitual tendencies and delusions. Practitioners can awaken to buddhahood through sadhana practice based on Tara.

Padmasambhava explains that there are untold numbers of Tara tantras. The ultimate source of these infinite Tara tantras, practices and teachings is the female dharmakaya buddha Samantabhadri. Vajra Yogini, among whose countless emanations at the nirmanakaya level is Tara, spread them into limitless realms. For our particular age, in recent times, all these tantras were condensed into three levels. The first, the extensive form, with an amazing number of teachings and rituals, was supposed to be revealed by the illustrious 19th-century master Jamyang Khyentse Wangpo. Unfortunately, due to a lack of auspicious coincidences, he never wrote down the instructions. He only retrieved the statue itself, which he recovered from a sacred location in the Zabbu valley of Shang in central Tibet and brought back to Kham.

The medium-length instruction, which Chokgyur Lingpa, a visionary master of the same period, revealed shortly afterwards, is called the *Zabtik Drölma, The Profound Essence of Tara*. It has several levels of practice: outer, inner and innermost. It is best known for its ritual of the four mandalas, which is widely practiced in hundreds of Dharma centers all over the world. Then there is the ultra-short instruction, which is the very core of this book. It is known as *The Essential Instruction on the Threefold Excellence*. It came about through the blessings of Samantabhadra, Vajra Yogini, Tara, and Padmasambhava with consort. When Chokgyur Lingpa saw Tara in a vision, she spoke three words: "*Lekso, lekso, lekso,*" which means "Excellent, excellent, excellent." Based on this, the meaning of the instruction that is the very core of this book appeared in his mind as a profound Dharma treasure.[1]

Some time later, Jamyang Khyentse Wangpo gave the transmission for this revealed treasure to his close friend and disciple, Jamgön Kongtrül, a master who was foretold by the Buddha and whose writings are unparalleled in their conciseness and clarity.

In this book we present the root text with two works of clarification—a pithy instruction by Tulku Urgyen Rinpoche, one of the greatest Dzogchen masters of recent times, and a longer, very practical guidance by Trulshik Adeu Rinpoche of Nangchen.

I feel we are incredibly fortunate that two recent masters who are holders of the lineage from Khyentse, Kongtrül and Chokling have given oral teachings on this text. It is with great joy that we share their wisdom with you, the reader. I wish that all of you receive the empowerment and instructions of Arya Tara and thereby receive her blessings, and that these blessings penetrate your lives and saturate everyone with whom you are connected.

—Erik Pema Kunsang
Nagi Gompa Hermitage, 2006

INTRODUCTION

Tara is an inspirational figure to many practitioners. She embodies the most compelling and vital qualities of the feminine: beauty, grace, and the ability to nurture, care for and protect. In addition, she is a true warrior, vanquishing fear and ignorance. One could say she is the earliest known Buddhist feminist.

We read in the *Vimalakirti Nirdesha Sutra*,[2] that Tara says:

> "In this life there is no such distinction as 'male' and 'female,' 'self-identity,' 'a person,' nor any perception (of such). Therefore, attachment to the idea of 'male' and 'female' is quite worthless. Weak-minded worldlings are continually deluded by this."

However, the sutra goes on to record the following vow by Tara:

> "There are many who wish to gain enlightenment in a man's form, and there are but few who wish to work for the welfare of sentient beings in a female form. Therefore, may I, in a female body, work for the welfare of beings until samsara has been emptied."

As Orgyen Tobgyal Rinpoche noted:

> "Tara's tenacity is immense. Buddha Shakyamuni vowed to awaken to enlightenment in the age when people's lifespan had degenerated to one hundred years. His resolve is considered superior to that of other buddhas. Buddha Shakyamuni himself, when teaching a sutra and a tantra on Tara, said that among all the other buddhas, Manjushri and Tara are the two who have exceedingly great resolve. Tara is like an emanation of the mother of all the buddhas

of the three times. She carries out all their activities, dispelling the obstacles created through the eight or sixteen types of fear. Most significantly, she vowed to emanate in female form until all of samsara is emptied. When anyone supplicates Tara, her response is swift. The activities resulting from her aspiration are extraordinary, and there is ample evidence of this, right up to the present day.

"Both Buddhists and non-Buddhists alike honor the divinity Jetsün Tara. There are quite a few traditions for her sadhana practice, not only in the sutras but also in the tantras. Each of the four levels of tantra, from Kriya to Anuttara, has its own distinct Tara practice."

Practitioners who wish to benefit beings and attain realization based on Tara need to garner the energy of this aspiration and apply it. Not only can we reach a level of personal achievement; we will be able to help the sick, safeguard the frightened and pacify mental suffering. It is a courageous journey to undertake.

Ordinary people do not question the commonly accepted version of reality. They conform to the standard values of subduing enemies and cherishing friends and family. Materialism, ambition and mundane achievements are the worldly hallmarks of success. We experience the phenomenal world and our minds as solid and truly existent. Very few people doubt these assertions and question their validity. Yet, the process of disbelief is the first step on the spiritual path.

Most of us come to the teachings from a place of dissatisfaction. Underlying our experience is a subtle uneasiness that we are unable to pinpoint. We have not totally bought into prevalent attitudes about the way things are. Instead, we are seeking to redirect our energy and revaluate our lives according to a different standard. We see so many levels and types of suffering, both physical and mental, and we wish for some way to alleviate this pervasive anguish, as well as our own discomfort.

If we are fortunate enough to follow these feelings all the way through, we will meet with a genuine teacher and a spiritual discipline that includes truthful self-examination, meditation and other skillful practices to disperse habitual negative patterns and assist the growth of positive ways of being.

An open mind and a willingness to seek alternative answers means we have moved in the right direction. We should enhance this approach by studying the histories and theories of these practices. We then carefully investigate the aspects of the different cycles of teachings to determine our particular path. Eventually, though, to bring about results, we need to embark on the training directly.

The results of work on ourselves can be painfully slow to come to fruition, while we have the wish to be able to help others at this very moment. Directing our attention toward those in trouble and practicing with them in mind will have a beneficial effect. We do not have to wait until we are fully accomplished to do this. No matter where we are on the path, we can help the unfortunate by taking Tara, for example, as our support.[3] Dzigar Kongtrül Rinpoche says, "Particularly, by taking refuge with another person in your visualization, you can benefit them immensely." Imagine what we can achieve through fully embodying Tara's qualities or even acquiring a little bit of them. When practicing *Zabtik Drölma,*[4] the extensive Tara sadhana elucidated in this book, we can place an unhappy or sick person right in our mental mandala and send them healing wishes. The blessings will be twofold, benefiting both them and us as well.

In Nepal, each monastery or nunnery is 'branded' with a practice that is considered its specialty. If a sponsor needs a certain activity energized, either dispelling or increasing, the word is out on where to go. The nunnery of Tulku Urgyen Rinpoche, Nagi Gompa, is known for the power of its Tara practice. There is a long line of people requesting the nuns to do Tara recitation. Whether it is the blessings of Tulku Urgyen Rinpoche or the blessings of the continual Tara practice, I do not know, but the nuns live comfortably. It is not of course a perfect place; there are the usual minor intrigues, but there are not so many problems. Most of the nuns are healthy, live long lives and dedicate themselves to Dharma practice with little hardship.

Deity practice is like receiving a light in a dark passage to guide us. It is through our inspiration and connection that we can open up to imbibe the essence of each deity. Through application of the skillful means of Vajrayana, we can achieve realization. When trying to accomplish a deity, we should always keep in mind that the qualities of each deity are simply those of our own basic buddha nature, fully manifested.

Adeu Rinpoche gave the following teaching, beginning with an explanation of the famous saying:

> "Even though there is no separateness in the expanse of dharmakaya, there is still a distinctness in the rupakaya, like individual rainbows appearing in the sky. Similarly, in the expanse of the dharmakaya of all buddhas, there is no difference whatsoever, yet the buddhas appear in different ways because of the various inclinations of sentient beings. The expansive wisdom mind is identical in all the buddhas. Out of this, they manifest various forms to benefit beings with individual proclivities and dispositions.

"There are many, many different means to influence beings, corresponding with their individual needs. These correspond to the inexhaustible adornment wheels of body, speech, mind, qualities and activities that manifest in innumerable varied fashions. In terms of enlightened activity, buddhas like Tara and Vajrakilaya appear to carry out all the buddha activities, including dispelling obstacles, removing fears, and providing whatever sentient beings need, pray and yearn for. The buddhas appear in particular forms to fulfill these diverse inclinations, which is why you find the specific manifestations of Tara, Vajrakilaya, and so forth. That is the general principle.

"If you then look back to the origin of Tara, way before manifesting at the time of enlightenment, she was simply someone who formed the specific resolve, the immense aspiration, to benefit sentient beings in the form of a female. In addition, in every rebirth consecutively from that moment until enlightenment, she vowed to be born as a female. Even though it is often said that enlightenment is not achieved in the form of a female, she still wanted to prove that it is not exclusive to the male form. You can find the story of Tara's past lives in a book by the great Tibetan master Taranatha, called the *Extensive Explanation of Tara*, which is actually a biography of Tara and her past lives.

"The special quality of Tara is her extraordinary compassionate resolve to benefit all beings by removing whatever causes them to feel anxious or afraid, and dispelling the eight or sixteen types of fears. There are two perspectives. One is that Tara was a practitioner on the path who first developed the ultimate supreme enlightenment, progressed on the path and finally awakened to buddhahood. Another perspective is that Avalokiteshvara's tears turned into Tara. How does one reconcile these two versions? That depends on the capacity of whoever is listening to the teachings. For ordinary people, the perspective of someone like oneself who progresses along the path is presented.

Yet, the true perspective is that in the Akanishtha buddhafield, all buddhas awaken to enlightenment, and then their emanation is seen as if attaining enlightenment in a world of ordinary beings. In actuality, there is no real conflict here between the two versions of the story. There are several versions of how the Buddha attained enlightenment according to different levels of teachings. It is like that. One is the relative perspective—you might say the superficial version—while the second is the ultimate, real perspective."[5]

Although the women among us might like to put Tara in the feminine camp and gain one for the girls' side, in doing so we show a lack of true understanding of how things really are. To quote Tulku Urgyen Rinpoche:

"The enlightened essence is present in everyone. It permeates all of samsara and nirvana, and appears in all sentient beings without exception. When we experience our enlightened essence and apply that in practice, we achieve enlightenment. The state of enlightenment knows no difference as to male and female."[6]

Tulku Urgyen continued,

"You can scan every single thing in this whole world and still not find an instruction superior to the one showing you how to recognize the nature of mind. It is the path that all past buddhas have traversed. Whoever awakens right now follows this path; all future buddhas will awaken by following this path. It is also called the Great Dharmakaya Mother, Prajñaparamita. This is not some sort of literal old lady. The Dharmakaya Mother is unconfined empty cognizance. The view of Prajñaparamita, as well as of the Great Middle Way, Mahamudra, and Dzogchen, are all views free of concepts. Present wakefulness is free of concept.[7]

Transcendent knowledge is beyond thought, word and
  description.
It neither arises nor ceases, like the identity of space.
It is the domain of individual, self-knowing wakefulness.
To this mother of the buddhas of the three times, I pay
  homage.

"Since transcendent knowledge is within the individual
domain of cognizant wakefulness, anyone can know
it. 'Domain' here means that it is possible to recognize.
What is recognized is not something that can be thought
of, described, or illustrated through an example. This
knowing itself is the mother of the buddhas of the three
times, Prajñaparamita, the Great Mother. The experience
quality of this is the male buddha, while the empty quality
is the female buddha. Their unity is the primordial Buddha
Samantabhadra with consort, also known as Changeless
Light.[8]

"The ultimate Dharma is the realization of the
indivisibility of basic space and awareness. That is the
starting point, and that is what is pointed out to begin with.
It is essential to understand this; otherwise, we might have
the feeling that Samantabhadra and his consort are an old
blue man and woman who lived eons ago. It is not like that
at all! Samantabhadra and his consort are the indivisible
unity of space and awareness,[9] or the inseparable unity of
emptiness and cognizance. Samantabhadra and his consort
are not confined to concepts such as male or female."[10]

There is enormously profound theory behind deity
practice.[11] The way to accomplish the deity is to combine the
recognition of mind essence with deity practice. Basically, we
engage in deity practice to clear away that which obscures
our ability to remain in the natural state. Because we are
on the path, we are by definition in a state of confusion. In

order to clear away our deluded perceptions, we use various spiritual practices that enable us to purify the obscurations and gather the accumulations, including the practices of visualization, recitation, and meditation. There are many explanations of the various Tara practices. However, *The Essential Instruction on the Threefold Excellence* is unique in that it outlines an entire path, taking Tara as support. *Skillful Grace* is a testament to this rich tradition. The book is divided into three main sections. The first is the root text of this cycle, *The Essential Instruction on the Threefold Excellence,* according to the mind treasure of *The Profound Essence of Tara* as revealed by Chokgyur Lingpa. Following that is a commentary on this root text by Tulku Urgyen Rinpoche. Next is Adeu Rinpoche's explanation, which synthesizes Jamgön Kongtrül's commentary on the same text.[12] In order to make this work less scholarly and more applicable to practitioners, we decided to paraphrase Jamgön Kongtrül's commentary and intermingle it with Adeu Rinpoche's teaching.

While working through the material presented in this book, we noticed an interesting melding of two styles of teaching in the commentaries by these two lamas.

The text here unfolds very closely to a statement Adeu Rinpoche made regarding how to point out the nature of mind to the two types of individuals:

> "Imparting the oral instructions for meditation practice requires an experienced guide, someone who has the blessings of a true lineage and who is aware of the individual capacity of the student. What is needed is someone who can 'take the pulse' of a student, so to speak, and decide what is necessary to bring the particular individual further along. Each student must be guided in accordance with his

or her individual ability. Each student needs a teacher who can fulfill his or her own personal needs. People are not the same: there are large differences from one person to the next, and so the instructions need to be individually adapted.

"Broadly speaking, there are two types of people: the gradual type and the instantaneous type; each of these needs to be given the pointing-out instruction in a different way. The gradual type of person needs to be guided step-by-step through the depths of meditation practice. The instantaneous type can have the nature of mind pointed out directly and immediately. This is in fact how it *has* to be. If the instantaneous style of instruction is given to someone who is not so sharp, it will go right over his or her head. On the other hand, if only the gradual instructions are given to an instantaneous type of person, they will not be satisfied; it will not be skillful for them, and the teachings will not click. To paraphrase a saying, 'For the instantaneous type, the gradual instructions are inadequate; while for the gradual type, the instantaneous type of teaching are inadequate.'

"This is why it is so important that a qualified meditation master gives progressive instructions to the gradual type and more direct instructions to the instantaneous type. Only a qualified master can correctly know which is required by the particular individual."

These different approaches are exemplified by these two masters' teachings. Tulku Urgyen Rinpoche presents the direct approach, while Adeu Rinpoche presents the progressive way. By studying both, we obtain a complete and full picture of how to put these instructions to use.

Every book has a life force and energy of its own, which unfolds as the project progresses. What became apparent in working with this material was its beauty, accessibility and ease of application. No matter where we are on the path, these instructions offer inspirational guidance. Many heartfelt thanks go to everyone involved in the making of this book: the transcriber, Elizabeth, the editor of the transcripts, Michael Tweed; the foreword author, Tara Goleman; the polish editor Kerry Moran, the typesetter Joan Olson; the proof reader Dr. Christine Daniels and the streamliner, Zack Beer. Finally without the continued support of Richard Gere of the Gere Foundation and his ever patient and professional executive director, Bob Kelty, this book might not have happened.

May we take as an example the realization, generosity and compassion of Jetsün Tara herself, as well as of Tulku Urgyen Rinpoche and Trulshik Adeu Rinpoche. Moreover, may we attain the ability to benefit beings in accordance with the most sublime precious mind of enlightenment in this very lifetime.

—Marcia Binder Schmidt

The Essential Instruction on the Threefold Excellence

Revealed by Chokgyur Lingpa

THE ESSENTIAL INSTRUCTION ON THE THREEFOLD EXCELLENCE

from

THE MIND TREASURE DRÖLMA ZABTIK THE PROFOUND ESSENCE OF TARA⁏

I bow at the feet of Arya Tara.⁏
Here are her gradual pith instructions,⁏
The oral instructions on the threefold excellence.⁏
Excellent, excellent, excellent—⁏
The tantra of the indestructible vajra nada,⁏
The inexpressible basis of all expression,⁏
Manifests in response to the aspirations of those to be
    tamed.⁏

The first excellence is the essential extract⁏
Of the vehicles for gods and humans, shravakas and
    pratyekabuddhas:⁏
The perfect trust and renunciation—⁏
The goodness at the beginning that is the instructions in
    the stepping stones for the path.⁏

The second excellence is the essential extract of
    Mahayana:⁏
Based on loving kindness and compassion,⁏
Perfect superior resolve is engendered ⁏
The goodness at the middle that is the instructions in
    the main practice.⁏

The last excellence is the essential extract of Secret
    Mantra:⁏

Based on development and completion,⁏
Perfect wisdom is engendered⁏
The goodness at the end that is the instructions in the
    concluding part.⁏

In order to practice these properly,⁏
Obtain empowerments, learn the crucial instructions⁏
And, with totally pure samayas and vows,⁏
Abandon all activities in a secluded place.⁏

Straighten the body and expel your stale breath.⁏
Scrupulously apply mindfulness⁏
And visualize your guru as Jetsün Tara.⁏
Supplicate one-pointedly and develop devotion.⁏
Mingle your mind with hers and remain in composure.⁏

Then, for the stages of the practice,⁏
Think of the freedoms and riches—so difficult to find
    and easy to lose,⁏
And of the sufferings of the lower realms.⁏
With trust in the unfailing results of karma,⁏
One-pointedly take refuge in Jetsün Tara⁏
Who embodies all objects of refuge, and keep the
    precepts.⁏

The three higher realms have nothing ⁏
Except the miseries of change and formation.⁏
So, with the intense renunciation of seeing the three
    worlds as a fire pit,⁏
Pursue the path of liberation.⁏
These were the preliminary stages of instruction.⁏

All suffering samsaric beings⁏
Are my kind mothers.⁏

Therefore, motivated by love and compassion towards
    each of them, ⁞
I will give my happiness and goodness to others ⁞
And take their suffering and its causes upon myself. ⁞
Beginning with your present mother, ⁞
Train your mind with everyone, throughout the
    universe. ⁞

In order to bring them happiness, ⁞
And dispel their suffering and its causes, ⁞
With the perfect superior intention, ⁞
Develop the aspiring awakened mind ⁞
And practice the six paramitas as application. ⁞

In particular, straighten your body, expel your stale
    breath. ⁞
Your focus, in the sky before you, is the form of Jetsün
    Tara, ⁞
Inseparable from your guru. ⁞
Envision her and visualize the emanation of light rays. ⁞

When dull, hold your mind on a sphere in her
    forehead, ⁞
When even, in her heart and, when agitated, at her
    navel. ⁞
Through unwavering concentration, ⁞
One-pointedly focus your mind, eyes and breath. ⁞
Finally, she dissolves into you. ⁞

Cut the pursuit of the thoughts of the three times. ⁞
Rest in the continuity of objectless naturalness. ⁞
With body and mind made pliable, shamatha is
    accomplished. ⁞
This is called the paramita of concentration. ⁞

Within this state, all that appears⸝
As outer and inner, the world and beings,⸝
Is merely personal perception, like dreaming.⸝
By looking towards the mind that perceives⸝
It is elusive and traceless, like a cloud in the sky.⸝
When carefully investigating your mind's nature,⸝
It is not manifold, but utterly empty.⸝
It is not a oneness, but vividly awake.⸝
In this state of indivisibility beyond concepts,⸝
Realize the samadhi of united shamatha and
        vipashyana—⸝
The ultimate Mother Jetsün Tara, Prajñaparamita.⸝
This was the instruction in the main practice of the
        path.⸝

After understanding that all phenomena are emptiness, ⸝
Train in unborn yet unconfined perception as the
        development stage.⸝

Externally, by the approach of gathering
        accumulations⸝
And internally, by the accomplishment of raining down
        blessings,⸝
Purify your being; while for the special innermost
        path,⸝
Visualize the guru yoga of devotion,⸝
Offer mandalas and supplications,⸝
Receive the four empowerments and mingle your
        minds.⸝

Then, for the great accomplishment,⸝
As the expression of the undivided three samadhis⸝

Visualize the mandala of the support and supported;⁞
And by vivid presence, stable pride,⁞
And pure recollection, accomplish clear visualization.⁞

By fully perfecting this distinctness⁞
That is capable of stopping clinging to ordinary
    experience,⁞
Apply the crucial points of body posture⁞
And focus your mind on a radiant sphere in the heart.⁞
When accustomed, rest without accepting or rejecting,⁞
Projecting or dissolving, in the continuity of original
    mind-essence.⁞

When some degree of wakefulness has dawned,⁞
Hold the vase with the union-breath⁞
And train the wind-path through vajra recitation.⁞

Once the channels and winds are made pliable,⁞
Use the contact with a qualified mudra⁞
To kindle the fire of great passion,⁞
Let the bliss descend, hold, turn, permeate and spread.⁞
Rest in the continuity of great wakefulness.⁞

As enhancement practices, light the tummo fire,⁞
And from TAM in the heart, emanate the light of OM,⁞
Through which the essences of the universe and beings⁞
Are gathered by HUNG and then absorbed.⁞
Focus the mind on the indestructible bindu⁞
And stabilize with breathing practice.⁞

Bring the immediate instant of self-existing awareness⁞
To basic space beyond conceptual mind.⁞
Through the illustrating example wisdom⁞

The real coemergent is realized,
And you accomplish Vajra Tara
Of the changeless three essences within this very life.

This was the gradual instruction on the concluding part
of the supreme path.

SAMAYA. SEAL, SEAL, SEAL. DATHIM.

Thus, having received the blessing of Jetsün Tara, Chokgyur Lingpa wrote this down as it flowed forth from the treasure mine of realization. ATIGUHYA.

AN OVERVIEW OF THE THREEFOLD EXCELLENCE

Tulku Urgyen Rinpoche

The Essential Instruction on the Threefold Excellence is from a *terma* or treasure root text. Among the various terma categories—mountain, rock, earth and wisdom-mind termas—this particular one is a mind treasure revealed by Chokgyur Lingpa. Chokgyur Lingpa went to a place where Padmasambhava had buried a terma of Jetsün Tara, and there had a vision that Tara said, *"Lekso, lekso, lekso,"* meaning "Excellent, excellent, excellent." Here I will explain that terma text.

The first verse of the text says, *the tantra of the indestructible vajra nada,* which verifies that these words are not ordinary, dualistically produced sound. *The inexpressible basis of all expression* is the sound of the unborn nature, which originates from the unconditioned speech of wisdom wind. This teaching is not fabricated through mundane, conceptual words. It *manifests in response to the aspirations of those to be tamed*: it appears to fulfill the wishes of disciples who are to be influenced.

The first excellence is the vehicles of gods, humans, shravakas and pratyekabuddhas. The teaching in the first excellence is on pure trust and renunciation. It is the virtue with which we must start, *the goodness at the beginning that is the instructions in the stepping stones for the path.* It is the instruction on the springboard for virtue that commences this practice, which includes purifying the obscurations and gathering the accumulations.

The second excellence covers the Mahayana teachings whereby, *based on loving kindness and compassion,* we develop a pure and superior intention. That is the intermediate virtue. It includes instructions on the main practice of the precious mind of enlightenment, the trainings in relative and ultimate bodhichitta, as well as instructions on shamatha and vipashyana.

The third excellence is composed of Vajrayana teachings. Both sutra and tantra are included, so that everything is complete. The third excellence is the essence of the Vajrayana path, which includes the practices of the development and completion stages. This is called the instruction on the last virtue, or the instruction on the subsequent practices. Also included here is training in Dzogchen. By practicing the inseparability of space and awareness, the path of *rigpa*, you accomplish Vajra Tara.

This instruction of *The Threefold Excellence* encompasses all practices necessary to attain complete enlightenment— outer, inner and secret practices. It embodies all three vehicles—Hinayana, Mahayana and Vajrayana. The instruction includes all nine yanas. There is nothing left out; it is totally complete.

> *In order to practice these properly,*
> *Obtain empowerments, learn the crucial instructions*
> *And, with totally pure samayas and vows,*
> *Abandon all activities in a secluded place.*

Apply mindfulness according to this particular exhalation practice. This means that the body should stay on the meditation seat, the mind should stay with the body, and looseness should stay with the mind.

Sitting on your meditation seat, visualize your guru in the form of Jetsün Tara. Pray to her with one-pointed devotion, giving rise to strong and fervent sincerity. After this, mingle your mind together with hers, and rest in composure. The guru's mind and your own mind become one.

Now come the four mind-changings to reflect upon. First is the difficulty of finding the precious human body, the riches and freedoms. It is extremely difficult to achieve, and even though we have temporarily found it, due to impermanence it is easily destroyed. Remember the suffering of the three lower realms and have confidence in the unfailing law of karma.

Next is refuge. Jetsün Tara is the embodiment of all objects of refuge, so with one-pointedness take refuge and keep the precepts, persist in the training. Remember that in the three upper realms there is the suffering of change and the all-pervasive suffering of karmic formation. The other three realms of samsara have the defects of all of samsara and are like being in a fire pit. Seeing this, give rise to renunciation and understand that samsara is pointless. Reflect on how the entirety of samsaric existence has no true joy but always a painful nature. Renunciation is to take to heart the futility of conditioned existence. There is nothing of value to pursue in samsara. It is completely useless not to strive for the path of liberation.

This was the instruction on the preliminaries and the teaching on the first excellence.

All suffering samsaric beings, suffering here means that in samsara, there is nothing stable or permanent, nothing beyond the pain of existence. Of all the beings in samsara, there is not a single one who has not been your own kind mother. Therefore, with the motivation of love and compassion toward all our parent sentient beings, *I will give my happiness and goodness to others / And take their suffering and its causes upon myself.* This practice is called *tonglen,* sending and taking. With our inhalation, we take in all the suffering of our mother sentient beings. With our exhalation, we transfer our happiness and wellbeing to others, to help ease their pain and eliminate the causes of it.

The way to develop compassion is as follows: imagine that you are bound and gagged and your mother of this life is dragged in front of you. As you helplessly watch, her body is cut open and her entrails spill out. The reaction you have at that moment is of tremendous grief and despair. This is compassion.

Next, try to expand this feeling of compassion to include not only your present mother, but all those who have been your mother in the past, beings as numerous as the sky is vast. The only difference between them is whether they are close or distant in time—whether they are alive now or they lived a long time ago. Every single one of them was your mother at some point in time. Thinking about all these beings, aren't you sad? *Beginning with your present mother, / Train your mind with everyone.* Train in this *to bring them happiness and dispel their suffering and its causes.* With the perfect superior pure thought, which is primarily compassion, *Develop the aspiring awakened mind / And practice the six paramitas as application,* which is the applied resolve. The bodhichitta of aspiration is the four immeasurables: loving kindness, joy, compassion and impartiality, while the bodhichitta of application is the six paramitas: generosity, discipline, patience, diligence, concentration and insight.

The third excellence starts after we have developed bodhichitta. It includes both development and completion stages. In particular, to begin, *straighten the body* and *expel your stale breath. / Your focus, in the sky before you, is the form of Jetsün Tara / Inseparable from your guru.* Picture her clearly, visualizing light rays emanating from her form. If she does not remain lucid, focus on a tiny sphere in her forehead. If you are balanced, focus on a sphere in her heart center. If you are agitated, restless or have many scattered thoughts, focus on a sphere in her navel. With unwavering concentration, one-pointedly direct your mind, eyes and breath towards Tara. *Finally, she dissolves into you.* This practice is both with and without focus. It includes instructions on how to improve the development stage practice by directing the gaze to various points on her body. It includes the eyes, the mind, and the breathing, as well as ways to alleviate agitation or dullness.

You can also retain the breath in a particular way so that the attention stays one-pointed. You can read about this in the commentary of Jamgön Kongtrül. Holding the breath and focusing the eyes and attention together is a way to tame the mind. The mind rides on the wild horse of the breath, so by holding it, you can control the mind. In other words, merge the breath and mind inseparably.

In actuality, there is not really a 'Tara' over there and a 'you' over here. Maintaining such concepts is the ordinary way of practicing. The text says, *Finally she dissolves into you*, meaning the visualized Tara melts into you and you become inseparable from her. This is the practice of the dissolution stage, where you remain nonconceptual. Then, *Cut the pursuit of the thoughts of the three times*—do not pursue any thought patterns. *Rest in the continuity of objectless naturalness*—relax effortlessly without any reference point. *With body and mind made pliable, shamatha is accomplished.* Then you will be able to accomplish a pliable body and mind, meaning the body can comfortably remain completely still all day long, and the mind will always stay in calm abiding. You become adept at this after practicing for a few years. *This is called the paramita of concentration*, transcendent serenity.

There are two kinds of calm abiding, shamatha. The first is with object or support, and the other is without an object. First, you visualize Tara; then remain without visualizing anything in the natural equipoise that is free of any object. Having stabilized this kind of calm abiding, *Within this state, all that appears / As outer and inner, the world and beings, / Is merely personal perception, like dreaming.* These individual occurrences are like experiences in our dreams. When dreaming, there is no substance to anything whatsoever, yet still the dream unfolds. We have a variety of feelings, but other people do not experience these phenomena. It is only our own phenomena taking place. Our experiences are our own displays.

The conventional view of reality postulates two types of experience: individual perceptions and commonly shared experience. Shared reality is whatever everyone experiences in common, the generally accepted truth—like water is water, earth is earth, this place is this particular place. When we die, this shared perception of reality comes apart. All that is left is our individual experiences and they are completely our own phenomena.

Actually, everything that appears and exists is already personal experience. As individuals, we deal with a deluded perception of what is. We think water is water, and earth is earth. An example of this is that when a yogi attains accomplishment, his experience and that of an ordinary person are completely different. Nothing can impede the yogi. All things, even the physical elements, are completely unobstructive. In his perception, everything is individually experienced as an illusion. Everything appears like one of the eight examples of the illusory nature of things.[13] In other words, everything is his own personal experience.

Because of the dualistic beliefs of sentient beings, the five colors of the basic nature appear as the five elements, and so forth. When this belief completely collapses, as it does for the yogi, then there is no obstruction whatsoever. Everything is merely the appearance of emptiness. All things are the self-phenomena of emptiness, possessing not even the slightest material nature. As long as we have not destroyed our dualistic beliefs, our clinging to the material substance of things, then the five elements of earth, water, air, fire and sky can obstruct us. Milarepa could fly in the sky and pass through rocks because he had no dualistic clinging left. To him, all phenomena appeared as illusory, because he had attained stability in self-existing wakefulness. It was not necessary for him to use force to physically penetrate through solid matter. He could simply pass through matter because his delusion had collapsed.

Samsara is created by nothing other than conceptual thought. Once thought has been destroyed, samsara has been destroyed. If samsara were real to begin with, it would be impossible to destroy. Because of our grasping, everything appears to be very substantial and solid. Once our delusion collapses and we realize that all things are insubstantial, we cannot be obstructed. We are able to traverse unimpededly through all phenomena, because the clinging to a solid reality has fallen away. Right now, we take what is unreal to be real and solid. We believe in our mistaken perception of reality, and are thus impeded and blocked. Our conditioned body, speech and mind obscure the unconditioned three kayas. The vajra body itself is unconditioned. Our bodies can be burnt by fire or washed away by water, but the vajra body, which is not born, cannot be burned.

The sutras mention something called 'twofold absence of identity.' When resolving this identitylessness, you must resolve the empty nature of the perceiver and perceived. The identitylessness of phenomena is to realize the lack of an identity in all perceived external objects. Realizing the lack of a self-entity in the inner perceiving mind is called the personal identitylessness. To resolve that the perceiver and the perceived, object and subject, have no real nature is to realize the twofold identitylessness.

Think about the conditioned nature of life. How can anything that is dependent upon other things be permanent? Life itself is conditioned; it has no permanence. Were our lives unconditioned to begin with, we could do whatever we want. But where in this life is there anything that lasts? Objects are merely perceptions; they have no true existence. All objects are the unreal, natural forms of emptiness. Perceptions or appearances themselves have no concrete existence. Only when our belief in appearances has been destroyed will appearances be beyond benefiting or harming.

It is said, "Mind is merely thoughts free from ground and root." What we call mind is just conceptual thinking, concepts moving to the five sense objects, conceptualizing them. Mind is nothing more than one thought moving after the other. Without an object, a thought cannot possibly move. Objects are simply defined as visible forms for the eyes, sounds for the ears, taste for the tongue, touch for the body and joy and sorrow for the mind. If we do not grasp at these objects, a thought cannot move since their movement depends on objects. Thoughts are linked to objects.

Internally there is the mind. Externally there are the five sense objects, while in between are the five sense organs and their five doors. These three components continuously link together in a seamless chain. The chain breaks once we realize identitylessness; but as long as it is not stopped, we are linked to samsara.

To reiterate, there is the outer perceived object and the inner perceiving mind. In the context of shamatha, the state of calm abiding, all outer and inner things—the world and beings, all personal phenomena—are like a dream. Outer beliefs have ceased. Even though it appears as if all things arise out of causes and conditions, in fact they are the expression of mind.

By looking towards the mind that perceives: now we come to the inner perceiving mind, looking inwardly and examining itself. How is it? *It is elusive and traceless, like a cloud in the sky,* meaning it is intangible. The movement of mind is seemingly there, even though it is not. It appears to be there, yet it is insubstantial. Just like a cloud in the sky, it emerges and then vanishes without a trace. The perceiving mind is no different—it is there, and yet it is not. When you look at it carefully, there is no trace of it. When a cloud disappears in the sky, it leaves no imprint on the place where it was. Nothing whatsoever remains.

The mind is the same way: though mind seems to be, it is empty. Though empty, it can be experienced—and yet it disappears, and does not remain. Another example for the perceiving mind is like a finger drawing on water. As you trace a design on the surface of the water, it disappears at the same moment. Likewise, you cannot say where the movements of the perceiving mind came from or where they go. Mental movements come and go; they arise, then completely and tracelessly disappear. That is the example.

When carefully investigating your mind's nature, once again, you have to look a little more closely. *It is not manifold, but utterly empty.* It is not many, which means it is not substantial, not concrete, not composed of numerous things. We have concluded that mind is not many. Rather, it is empty like space—completely open, unobstructed, and substanceless. *It is not a oneness, but vividly awake.* The clarity of the mind is like the sun rising in the sky, illuminating everything. We cannot say that mind is only one, empty, or nothing, because it is a clear wakefulness that is like the rays of the sun. The emptiness and the wakefulness are indivisible—they are not two different things. This indivisibility is called *rangjung yeshe*, the self-existing wakefulness that is completely beyond the grasp of intellectual thought.

It is never said that you see the buddha nature by means of intellectual ideas.

The mind's indivisibility of being empty and awake, the continuity of that, is here called the unity of shamatha and vipashyana. *Realize the samadhi of united shamatha and vipashyana / The ultimate Mother Jetsün Tara, Prajñaparamita.* Whether you say Great Mother Dharmakaya, Samantabhadri, or Prajñaparamita, it is the real Tara. From the dharmakaya, the sambhogakaya unfolds as Vajra Varahi, and from that, Jetsün Tara manifests as the nirmanakaya. This refers to the inseparability of the unconfined empty and wakeful state, beyond ideas.

This was the instruction on the main practice of the path.

The more detailed teaching is the third excellence, which starts with the line, *After understanding that all phenomena are emptiness.* This means knowing things to be as they are. All phenomena are the unity of appearance and emptiness. Everything is not merely a nothing. In the Sanskrit word *shunyata*, *shunya* means empty, and *ta* means present or aware. You can also say that shunyata is the unity of appearance and emptiness. All things are perceptible yet empty; they appear while being empty and are empty while appearing. Everything has the quality of emptiness. 'Empty and awake' means that the nature of everything is unborn, without obstruction, without limitation. This nature is not born, just as space is not born like a child is from its mother's womb.

If there is no being born, there is also no ending. If everything were merely a blank nothingness, this cessation would remain vacant, empty. Phenomena are empty of inherent reality, yet they appear without any obstruction. If we think that things are only empty, we would limit ourselves to a blank emptiness similar to physical space, which has no consciousness; it is neither confused nor liberated. It is mere matter. Buddha nature, however, is unconfined. It is not restricted to being either empty or awake. It is unborn and unconfined, because when there is no birth there is no cessation. Being unborn is the sign of being empty, and being unhindered is the sign of having wakefulness.

Wakeful while being empty, and empty while being wakeful—there is no obstruction to either. If there were some kind of obstruction, reality would stay only empty or only awake, but that is obviously not how we are and how we experience. Due to the openness of empty space, things can emerge. If there were not this unobstructedness, then earth, water, fire and wind would not be able to come about. In actuality they do appear; they are formed and dissolve in space. The same goes for the mind that is unborn and unceasing—it is not stuck. It is naturally beyond the two confines of permanence and nothingness, and the beliefs in eternalism and nihilism. Recognizing the indivisibility of appearance and emptiness saves you from being stuck in either of these two extremes. Here, the apparent aspect of this unborn and unceasing nature is the development stage. It is this wakeful aspect you should train in.

Train in unborn yet unconfined perception as the development stage. Forms, sounds, tastes, smells and sensations are perceived by the sense organs. Perception refers to the forms and sights experienced by the eyes, the sounds heard by the ears, the tastes experienced by the tongue, the smells by the nose, and the sensations experienced by the body. You should transform these perceptions into the development stage.

To develop means to make. The ultimate sense of the meaning is that appearances arise from the continuity of emptiness. They are the unity of emptiness and awareness. From this state of suchness, everything manifests unimpededly. That which is unborn and unfabricated is not mentally invented: it is the basis of what is already there, the innate nature. The lama introduces the innate nature to you. While remaining in that, allow the mandala to unfold.

If you are unable to do so, then, after letting be in empty awareness, when a mental movement occurs, transform this thought by reflecting, "Here is a celestial palace!"

All the thoughts and appearances that arise can become the development stage when you change them into pure manifestations, meaning the buddha's palace, deities, and so on.

Vajrayana practice has four branches: approach, full approach, accomplishment and great accomplishment. While training in the development stage, to externally accumulate merit is called the approach, together with internally accumulating merit through the consecration. To receive the blessings of the deity is called the accomplishment. These outer and inner points, accumulating merit and receiving the blessings, purify your nature.

For the special innermost path, *visualize the guru yoga of devotion.* Meditate on the guru yoga, *offer mandalas and supplications, / Receive the four empowerments and mingle your minds,* with your teacher's.

Then, for the great accomplishment, Next we come to the aspect of great accomplishment during which we train in the three samadhis. These are all complete within the 'mandala abiding as the ground.' The first samadhi is the samadhi of suchness—the great emptiness, rigpa, introduced to you by your teacher. However, if you have not recognized rigpa and need to fabricate, think that everything from form up to omniscience is complete emptiness without any concrete identity. The true nature of suchness is the original state that is totally untampered with, unchanged in any way. This is the self-knowing wakefulness. When the teacher introduces you to your nature, you do not need to fabricate in any way whatsoever. The lama does not introduce you to a suchness that needs to be created; he or she simply points out that which does not arise, dwell or cease. The actual suchness samadhi is the original state, free from arising, dwelling or ceasing.

The second samadhi is the all-illuminating samadhi, also known as the samadhi of great compassion. In the state of recognizing rigpa, there is a natural compassion that is intrinsic to this state, just as water is naturally wet. Being unfabricated, this compassion does not have to be created in any way. Simply by remaining in the true nature, compassion genuinely wells up. If you have not recognized rigpa, then you must give rise to compassion by thinking of all the poor sentient beings that do not understand emptiness.

The third samadhi is the samadhi of the seed syllable. It is the emptiness of the first inseparable from the compassion of the second. It unfolds in the form of a seed syllable.

As the expression of the undivided three samadhis, / Visualize the mandala of the support and supported. The support is the buddha palace while the supported is the deity, in this case Jetsün Tara. 'Visualize' refers to the development stage, which has three points: vivid presence, stable pride and pure recollection.

Vivid presence means visualizing the features of the central deity distinctly and clearly, down to the pores of the body and the colors of the eyes. Vivid presence is when all the details stand out crisp and clear. Stable pride is the firm confidence, completely free from doubt, that "I am the deity"—in this case Jetsün Tara. Pure recollection is to remember the meaning of the symbolism. For example, the two eyes of the deity represent insight and skillful means, the two arms and legs are the four immeasurables, the single face represents the single sphere of dharmakaya, and so on. All the details of the deity symbolize something pure.

These three are also called vividness, firmness and purity: vividness of form, firmness of pride and purity of recollection. *By fully perfecting this distinctness / That is capable of stopping all clinging to ordinary experience,* your mundane perceptions—of the outer universe, of sentient beings, and of clinging to pleasure, pain and sensations—are all brought to a halt. Visualizing a deity can completely cease all clinging to the concreteness of reality.

When you have completely brought these three aspects to perfection, when the vividness is completely crisp and clear, you apply the Anu Yoga practices of the body postures as well as training in the channels, energies and essences.

Next, *focus your mind on a radiant sphere in the heart. When accustomed, rest without accepting or rejecting, / Projecting or dissolving, in the continuity of original mind-essence.* Mind-essence means the indivisibly empty and awake state. Original continuity means uninterrupted naturalness. Rejecting means thinking, "These thoughts don't belong in the view; I must get rid of them." Accepting means, "I must get this awareness. It *must* be acquired." Completely drop both accepting and rejecting. Then there can be the openness of awareness, rigpa. Through naturalness, you recognize the state that is identical with the first samadhi, the samadhi of suchness.

When some degree of wakefulness has dawned, in other words, by practicing for some time and becoming accustomed to this, to some extent, original wakefulness will dawn. When this happens, train in the 'union-breath.' Union-breath refers to the vase-shaped breathing, which is a technique of holding the breath in a very specific way. After that, you continue training in the *prana* path with the vajra recitation. This recitation is not by means of the mouth, but done mentally while training with the breath.

Once the channels and winds are made pliable, meaning workable, and you have gained independence or mastery in the structured channels, the moving winds and the arranged essences, *Use the contact with a qualified mudra,* look for a qualified consort. If you are a woman, find a male partner, if a male, find a female. The root of the practice is how to let the bliss descend, be held, turned, permeated and spread, while all the time letting be in the continuity of the great wakefulness. Thus, *To kindle the fire of great passion, / Let the bliss descend, hold, turn, permeate and spread. / Rest in the continuity of great wakefulness.*

As an enhancement practice, sometimes *light the tummo fire.* Then radiate light from the mantra and gather all the essences. Emanate the radiance of OM TARE TUTTARE TURE SOHA in the heart center around the TAM, the seed syllable in the heart center. This is the recitation. Through this, the essences of the universe and beings are gathered and absorbed by the HUNG.

Focus the mind on the indestructible bindu. This is the absolute bindu; it is not of material substance. The indestructible essence is not something material; it is the awareness or dharmakaya itself. *And stabilize with breathing practice.* This practice of holding the breath while visualizing demonstrates the inseparability of energy-wind and mind. Practices that hold some type of object or reference point still have a relative sense to them. Elaborate practices like visualizing, holding of the union-breath, doing tummo, emanating and absorbing are all relative practices in this sense. However, through them, you can realize the absolute.

Bring the immediate instant of self-existing awareness / To basic space beyond conceptual mind: this is the ultimate practice. To let awareness pervade space is to bring the moment of self-existing awareness into inconceivable space. It is the practice of remaining in the continuity of mingled space and awareness, recognizing the view or training in self-existing awareness.

Through the illustrating example wisdom, the example wisdom demonstrates that you realize the absolute wisdom, the inseparability of space and awareness. Here it is called *coemergent. And you accomplish Vajra Tara / Of the changeless three essences within this very life.* The changeless three essences are the essences of nadi, prana and bindu. The essence of nadi is the wisdom channel, the essence of prana is the wisdom wind, and the essence of bindu is the wisdom sphere. Actually, all three are simply original wakefulness. Ultimately, the three changeless essences are the original wakefulness that is immovable and unchanging. Whatever changes or moves is a thought or stirring of the mind. Whatever is immovable is rigpa, awareness itself, original wakefulness.

This was the gradual instruction on the concluding part of the supreme path. SAMAYA. SEAL, SEAL, SEAL. DATHIM.

Thus, having received the blessing of Jetsün Tara, Chokgyur Lingpa wrote this down as it flowed forth from the treasure mine of realization. ATIGUHYA

Jamgön Kongtrül wrote a commentary on this root text. Upon completion, he said that if he had to write a complete explanation on this teaching that condenses all the methods of both sutra and tantra, it would take a massive volume. However, condensing it too much would make it impossible to understand. Therefore, he made it a medium-length commentary.

SKILLFUL GRACE

Trülshik Adeu Rinpoche

INTRODUCTION

Please form the resolve set upon attaining supreme enlightenment for the benefit of all sentient beings, who are as numerous as the sky is vast, and continue to read while maintaining such an attitude.

From the start, every practice requires three steps: learning, reflection and application. To begin with, we need to receive the teachings in an authentic way. Real learning involves gaining understanding about an instruction. To do this, we need to hear it clearly from someone who is part of a living tradition. That person needs to have a true transmission for the teaching, and must be able to pass it on clearly.

Having received the teaching, we then need to ponder it for ourselves. We need to gain some confidence and conviction about the value and methods of the teaching.

Finally, we need to put the teaching to use by familiarizing ourselves with the practice and integrating it into our life. That is the only way practice can truly take effect and become an actuality. To simply know about a teaching and not use it does not work. Mere intellectual knowledge is insufficient. It is the same as trying to cure a disease by simply reading about medicine, or by setting the medicine out on a table and looking at it, but not taking it. No one has ever been cured by merely looking at a bottle of medicine—you must take it. We must apply the treatment. All teachings are meant to be applied.

After intellectually understanding a teaching and establishing it with certainty, it is vital to clear up any misconceptions and doubts you may have about it. Then you must make use of it in a very personal and intimate way, by practicing. This final point is where any teaching becomes effective—by actually practicing it, not simply knowing about it.

All the masters of both the Kagyü and Nyingma lineages have agreed that for a beginner on the spiritual path, compassion, devotion and renunciation do not come naturally from one moment to the next. It simply does not happen like this at first. You must begin by forming the attitude of compassion, devotion and renunciation, and deliberately training in these. Over time, compassion, devotion and renunciation will come more and more naturally, in a non-natural and uncontrived way.

Renunciation, the will to be free, is a quality that every Dharma practitioner needs in order to progress on the path. Without it, you will not move forward. The first part of the general preliminaries helps to nurture the wish to be free. The four mind-changings involve facing some unavoidable facts, so that you do not want anything other than freedom, and you detach from samsaric aims very naturally. That is why the preliminaries are so vital to become a genuine Dharma practitioner. In Tibet, there is a saying about a person who wants to be a Dharma practitioner, but who has no sense of detachment from samsara. That person is said to be like someone who builds a many-storied house on a frozen lake in the dead of winter. The structure may seem very solid, but when spring comes and the lake thaws, the whole building sinks. Similarly, you may have a bit of apparent steadiness in your practice, but without renunciation, as soon as difficulties or hardships arise, your practice crumbles. That is why Dharma practitioners should focus from the very beginning on detachment and renunciation, the will to be free.

In the past in Tibet, instruction manuals were designed in such a way that practitioners who started the preliminaries only received teachings on the first part. The teachings were then stopped until the students completed their practice. Teachings resumed when the student returned for the next instruction. After getting that instruction, students would go off and practice it, and so on, until they had completed both the general and specific preliminaries. Everything was not freely given in advance, and there was no assumption that you could practice at your own whim. No practice, no instructions. The same method was used for the development stage of the yidam deity: you would receive instructions for a particular part of the practice, and then train in it. Having completed that, you came back for more instructions. To receive instructions on Dzogchen or Mahamudra required at the very least that you'd completed the preliminaries.

That is how it used to be in Tibet. These days it appears to be a bit different. Many people want to skip everything and go directly to the completion stage. There are also those who, without having done any yidam practice or preliminaries, immediately want to do the yogic practices involving the subtle channels and energies. I, however, have great doubts about the effectiveness of such an approach—whether any actual understanding is developed, and whether this type of method is authentic and correct. Still, many people would like to jump ahead, skipping all the steps in between.

The Buddhist path is laid out in a progressive order from the very beginning, and there is a particular reason for this. Having taking the first step, it is much easier to take the next because you are already a little ways along. Having completed the first step of the practice, you have already reached a certain level of accomplishment, so you are ready to move on to the next level. It is relatively simple to take the next step. That is why it was designed in this way.

If people do not want to respect this system and try to skip ahead to unfamiliar places, difficulties will most likely occur. You may receive a particular teaching, but you will need to apply it in practice. And I can guarantee that it will not be that easy to do so. It does not mean that it is impossible, but it requires a tremendous amount of perseverance, and it is questionable whether such a type of person is actually willing to apply the necessary time and energy to the practice. It could be that after a while you find that nothing has happened, that you have not accomplished anything. At this point, it is quite easy to blame the teachings for not getting you anywhere, when in fact your impatience is to blame. Therefore, going step-by-step from the beginning is probably more beneficial in the end.

Many students do have a sincere interest in Dharma practice. Please understand that guru yoga is one of the most important of the preliminary practices. It is through guru yoga that we receive the blessings for the true transmission of realization. After reciting the supplications, receiving the four empowerments, and mingling your mind with your teacher, you receive the blessings that enable you to connect with the view of the completion stage, which is not something that you can jump into without receiving an explanation. This is strongly emphasized in the Nyingma School. There is a traditional saying from the great masters:

Realization is reached through the path of blessings.
Blessings are reached through the path of devotion.
Devotion is reached through the path of supplication.

In other words, you cannot simply connect with the state of realization without any preparation. To realize original wakefulness, you need to connect with it through blessings, and blessings depend upon your own devotion, openness and trust. You can cultivate these qualities through supplication, by bringing to mind the great qualities of your master, known as 'the inexhaustible adornment wheel of the master's qualities,' and articulating your devotion in the form of a prayer or supplication. That is how devotion is brought forth, as well as how you receive the blessings and gain realization.

Jigten Sumgön, the great Drigung Kagyü master known as 'the lord of the three levels of existence,' wrote this verse:

Unless the sunshine of your devotion
Strikes the snow mountain of the guru's four kayas
The streams of blessing will not flow—
So, persevere in the practice of devotion.

Please recognize that if you want to realize the four kayas of the state of realization, you need to persevere in the openness of devotion; otherwise, it will not happen.

The Kagyü chant to Vajradhara, known as the *Dorje Chang Chungma,*[14] says, "Devotion is the head of meditation, as is taught." The most important part of the body is the head: without the head of devotion, there can be no meditation training. The Indian siddha Saraha wrote a verse that said:

> Only through clearing the veils and by creating merit,
> And by receiving blessings of a master, most sublime,
> You realize the coemergent, the pristine and timeless wisdom;
> Know therefore as delusion every other method's way.

Employing any other method to realize the state of original wakefulness, such as trying to figure out on your own what your basic nature is by using concepts, is simply folly. The only path is that of blessings and devotion to a qualified master.

In the teachings of the Drukpa Kagyü lineage, there are 'four sealed teachings.' The first one is the view, which is Mahamudra. Second is the meditation, which is the six doctrines of Naropa. Third is the conduct, which is the six cycles of equal taste, and the fourth is the sevenfold instruction on auspicious coincidence that is said to be the ever-important guru yoga. Guru yoga is indispensable at every single level of the path. In the Drukpa Kagyü teachings, there is another saying, "It is questionable whether you can be liberated through meditation, but there is no doubt that you can be liberated through devotion." Of course, it is possible that someone could meditate and thereby become liberated, but the result is not guaranteed. However, if you meditate with devotion to your guru, then there is no doubt that you will be liberated.

Guru devotion and the practice of the guru sadhana are strongly emphasized in the Nyingma teachings. Padmasambhava said, "To realize the guru is to realize the state of all the sugatas." This means that "If you realize me," his basic nature, "you realize the nature of all the buddhas" because he is the nature of all buddhas. This is why the guru sadhana is found among the termas of every single major *tertön*.

The heart of the Buddhist path is training in the original wakefulness, the state of equanimity, which is the basic meditation state itself. This is what we need to grow used to, and this is what the pointing-out instruction is all about. Your root guru bestows the pointing-out instruction, because, simply put, no one else knows how to do it. The one who can point out the nature in actuality is your vajra master. Thus, if you emphasize training in guru sadhana and guru devotion even before receiving the pointing-out instruction, it will have tremendous benefit.

Before we accept someone as our teacher and guide, all the scriptures including the Vajrayana tantras say that we need to examine whether that person is qualified to be a master. Blind acceptance of a teacher could be as harmful as unwittingly drinking a poison. This is not only from the student's point of view. The lama must also examine whether the student is qualified as well, or else it could be like jumping off a precipice into an abyss. It is necessary for *both* teacher and student to be truly qualified.

In addition, the instruction must be potent; it must be a qualified instruction. If these factors are complete, then the outcome will be authentic and perfect. It is important to clarify all of this before entering any kind of relationship with a Vajrayana teacher. It is not good enough to follow someone before finding out, because there are those who will lead you in the wrong direction if you just follow along blindly. It is our own responsibility to check all this carefully first. This point is stated repeatedly in the teachings, and it is traditional to check beforehand. If not, we may find out that the teacher we have been following is not qualified, like discovering that the drink we imbibed was poisonous.

Likewise, the teacher needs to determine that the student is willing to apply the teachings in a thorough way, and that he or she has the fortitude, courage, compassion, intelligence and renunciation to carry through. The individual might only be someone who is out 'musk hunting,' trying to get hold of a particular teaching in order to use it for selfish aims. Teachings are wasted on someone who never really applies them, and entering into such a relationship can be like jumping into an abyss. Both the teacher and the student can end up in one of the hell realms. We must be extremely careful in entering a teacher-student relationship. Since this point is mentioned in all the scriptures, maybe it is important!

In the context of the cycle of teachings explained in this book, when you practice the guru sadhana, you should regard Tara as being indivisible from your own root guru. Whoever your guru might be in essence, there is no difference between him or her and Tara. While you may not initially feel complete reverence and devotion, you must try to develop it. In the beginning, devotion may be artificial but through the practice of opening up, you should get to the point where you appreciate that the guru's nature is identical to that of all the buddhas of the three times. However, in terms of kindness towards you, your guru's kindness is even greater. Once you have developed that kind of devotion within your guru yoga practice, you are said to have established a firm foundation for the main practice of Mahamudra or Dzogchen.

Now I will begin explaining a text, which is a terma

revealed by the great tertön Chokgyur Dechen Lingpa. It is called the *Lekso Sumgyi Döntri, The Essential Instruction on the Threefold Excellence,* which includes a sadhana of Tara. I first received an explanation on this text from Samten Gyatso, the root guru of Tulku Urgyen Rinpoche, then again from Dzongsar Khyentse Chökyi Lodrö. Later I received it once more from the retreat master Sherab Lobzang, as well as from the previous incarnation of Tsoknyi Rinpoche. This present book is based on the commentary written by Jamgön Kongtrül.[15]

Both Sarma and Nyingma, the old and the new schools, have Tara practices corresponding to the various levels of tantra. There are many Tara sadhanas in the new schools, and many Nyingma tertöns have revealed Tara practices as well. For instructions on how to do Tara practice, there may perhaps be a text more detailed than the *Lekso*, but I do not know of one. Thus, for those who want to do Tara practice, there is probably no instruction superior to this; it is utterly complete. It has all the preliminaries, as well as the main part, which is divided into outer sadhana, inner sadhana, and innermost sadhana, as well as the subsequent yogas, and so forth. You can practice whichever is appropriate—the outer sadhana with Tara, or the inner with the twenty-one Taras that dispel the various fears, or the innermost practice of Tara with consort. The *Lekso* has all the details on the development stage, and describes the completion stage both with and without conceptual attributes. Even though some of the final yogas, such as the Subsequent Yoga, are mentioned quite briefly, I feel that they are still included so that nothing is left out. You can be confident that this is an entirety of instruction, covering everything from beginning to end. It is very difficult to find a Tara practice more complete than this.

The teachings I will discuss contain general topics of Dharma practice as well as the innermost view and meditation of Vajrayana, which is something of immense value. The goodness of this is beyond measure. It is impossible to estimate the far-reaching value of aiming our minds in that direction, taking delight in and wanting to involve ourselves in practicing and realizing the Dharma. This is an incredible goodness. Yet, many, many beings lack such good fortune. They are temporarily cut off from the kind of good circumstances we enjoy right now. We should thus dedicate the merit—both the general merit and that of being involved in the innermost Vajrayana—to all sentient beings who have been our own kind mothers in past lives. May they too have the good fortune to meet the sublime teachings and be benefited. Exemplified by that goodness, at the end of any Dharma session or teaching, dedicate to sentient beings every type of merit that has possibly been formed. This also insures that any benefit we have accrued will not go to waste or dissipate, and will not be damaged in any way whatsoever. Due to the enlightened attitude of bodhichitta, this dedicated merit becomes inexhaustible.

Historical Background

Jamgön Kongtrül begins his commentary with a sentence in Sanskrit, which means "Homage to the guru indivisible from Arya Tara."

The next four lines are an opening verse in which Jamgön Kongtrül pays respect by praising Tara's qualities and resolve. Of course, all buddhas and bodhisattvas have resolved to attain complete enlightenment to benefit every single sentient being. However, there is something unique about Arya Tara's resolve, in that she vowed that until complete awakening, she would always incarnate in the female form. Here, Jamgön Kongtrül praises Tara's determination and compassion as being more wonderful than that of all the buddhas and bodhisattvas, so therefore he asks her, "Please protect me until I gain complete enlightenment."

The next four lines contain Jamgön Kongtrül's pledge to complete what he is going to write. He also describes what the text is about, namely, the tantras from Tara. There is not merely one: they are immeasurable, like an ocean. In this commentary, Jamgön Kongtrül has written a condensation of the most vital essence of all of them—the profound, essential realization of Tara—in a way that is complete and concise. This is the type of guidance text that he decided to write, the quintessence of all the teachings, which brings supreme realization in a single lifetime.

Jamgön Kongtrül says, "I would like to start by briefly mentioning the historical background connected to this teaching." Then he goes into a narration of Tara's incarnations. Connected to Tara there are countless tantras, sadhanas, and pith instructions present in all the buddhafields. Many of those existing in our realm come through the emanation of Avalokiteshvara known as Padmasambhava. He came to Tibet and gave the instructions in both detailed and concise forms, suitable for the king of Tibet, his companion, Yeshe Tsogyal, and his close disciples. But most of his teachings on these tantras, pith instructions and sadhanas were meant for future times, and so were concealed in the form of mind termas, earth termas, sky termas, and so forth. All of these taken as a whole form one set of Tara teachings.

Yeshe Tsogyal left the human realm for the celestial realm at the valley of Shang Zabbu, and that is where this Tara terma was concealed. Jamyang Khyentse Wangpo was supposed to go there and reveal it, but he did not succeed in doing so. Instead, he revealed various types of mind treasures. The most important and profound of these connected with the *Lekso* is the *Chimey Pagma Nyingtik*. Chokgyur Lingpa had another treasure, linked to *Barchey Künsel*, called the *Four Deities for Dispelling Obstacles*, of which Tara is the first of the four deities. It has many sadhana activities associated with it. However, the most special terma, the quintessence, is the *Zabtik Drölma*, *The Profound Essence of Tara,* which is practiced today in Buddhist centers all over the world.

At the end of the Dark Age, Chokgyur Lingpa appeared as the undisputed and universally accepted tertön, the guide of beings. He went to one of the twenty-five sacred places of eastern Tibet connected to the Enlightened Speech of Qualities, which is the Lotus Crystal Cave.[16] While staying there, one morning at dawn he had a vision of Arya Tara appearing before him saying, "Lekso," meaning "excellent," three times in a row. Due to receiving this blessing, these profound and concise teachings completely overflowed from within the expanse of his realization. Having established the text in writing, he gave it to Jamyang Khyentse Wangpo in a one-to-one transmission lineage. The real owner of the teaching was therefore Jamyang Khyentse, whose tertön name was Pema Ösel Do-Ngak Lingpa. Jamyang Khyentse was the one who was supposed to reveal these teachings, but because he never had the opportunity to go to the valley of Shang Zabbu, Chokgyur Lingpa gave it to him before any other person.

Jamgön Kongtrül explains, "My lord guru Pema Ösel Do-Ngak Lingpa practiced this for three years, after which he graciously bestowed it upon me. That is how I received it." That was the historical background in brief. Here is a concise overview of the contents of the terma: it includes first the empowerment, then the outer, inner, and innermost sadhanas, the supreme activities, and finally the cycle connected to the guardian of the teaching.

STEPPING STONES FOR THE PATH: HINAYANA

This terma root text, *The Essential Instruction on the Threefold Excellence*, contains teachings of the three times that were expressed as a tantra of the indestructible vajra *nada*, the sound which is both inexpressible and the basis for all expression that appears in accordance with the inclinations of those to be influenced.

Repeating 'excellent' three times has a specific meaning. It symbolizes the goodness at the beginning, which is the instructions that are the stepping stones for the path; the goodness of the middle, which is the basis for the path itself; and finally the goodness of the end, which is the main part of the path. There are instructions connected to each of these three aspects.

The term 'stepping stones for the path' refers to how to arrive in 'the truly high and the definite goodness,' which refers to gods, human beings and the state of liberation and enlightenment. The stepping stones for shravakas and pratyekabuddhas are primarily faith and renunciation, and are called the gradual path for the individuals of lesser and medium capacity.

We personally apply these steps in two types of preliminaries: the preliminaries for the session, and the preliminaries for the teaching.

Preliminaries for the Session

First, sit in a place that is free from meditation thorns. 'Meditation thorns' means anything that takes you away from the practice—anything that distracts, interrupts, or is a hindrance to practice. Go to a place where there are no interferences of any kind and give up all deluded activities connected to body, speech and mind. Sit down on a comfortable seat with crossed legs and straight back. You can sit in the peaceful posture of mental ease, the sevenfold posture of Vairochana, or any other posture that is comfortable, as long as you maintain a straight back. Exhale three times the stale breath that is connected to the three poisons. Then simply relax the mind undistractedly. In other words, pay attention to the teachings that follow.

Full of faith and trust, imagine that in the sky before you, upon a lotus flower resting on a moon disc, sits the one who is in identity your own root guru, but looks like Arya Tara, the embodiment of all objects of refuge in a single form.

While picturing this in your mind, repeat,

Glorious guru, indivisible from sublime and Arya Tara,
    I supplicate you.
Please bestow your blessings upon me.
Please pacify every type of defilement and incorrect
    thinking.
Please allow the true realization to dawn in my mind.

Please eliminate every hindrance for accomplishing the
teachings of the Mahayana.

Continue chanting this prayer repeatedly, until true
devotion wells forth in your heart and mind.

As I mentioned earlier, devotion is not necessarily a
natural and spontaneous occurrence right from the start.
The instructions on guru yoga in some texts state that first
we supplicate, next we expand, and then finally we receive
blessings. In the beginning, we should think about whom
we actually are, ponder our traits and admit to ourselves
that we are not very special. Then, comparing our inferior
characteristics to the great qualities of the guru, we will
develop increasing admiration and trust. When this becomes
spontaneous and deeply heartfelt, tears will come to our eyes
and the hairs on our body will stand on end. That is how we
enter the blessings. Upon receiving the blessings, devotion
will become even deeper, and we will receive even more
blessings. Do not to expect to have complete and sincere
devotion from the very first. Until true devotion arises
genuinely, you need to create a facsimile of devotion at the
beginning of each session. Over time, the habit of devotion
will become more and more natural.

As your devotion grows stronger and stronger, imagine
that your guru comes down through the crown of your head
and settles in a sphere of light in your heart center. Make the
decision to dedicate the virtuous roots created through your
practice toward all sentient beings, so that they may attain
complete and perfect enlightenment. In this way, dedicate
the merit.

This sequence—visualizing the guru, supplicating, then
dissolving the guru through the crown of your head down

into the heart center and dedicating—should come at the beginning of every meditation session.

PRELIMINARIES FOR THE TEACHING

The preliminaries for the teaching are primarily meant for people of lesser and medium capacity. These preliminaries consist of four contemplations—the difficulty of obtaining the freedoms and riches; death and impermanence; the suffering of the lower realms; and the consequences and causes of karmic actions—along with taking refuge.

At the beginning of each of these contemplations, we repeat the visualization, supplication and dissolution of the guru into our heart center. After that comes the contemplation itself.

The Precious Freedoms and Riches

To begin with, think of everything we have—our success, our property, our possessions, and so on. Next, compare these to the most important basis for being able to practice the Dharma, which is the freedoms and riches that are extremely difficult to find. There is nothing more valuable than the perfect opportunity to practice; we *are* afforded that right now. We have obtained what is extremely difficult to obtain, the precious human body. Do not let it go to waste.

In the sutra called *The White Lotus of Compassion*,[17] the Buddha says, "It is extremely difficult to be reborn as a human, and even more so to have the perfect freedoms." It is not easy for a Buddha to appear in the world. It is not easy to decide to practice the true Dharma. In addition, it is extremely complicated to achieve perfect aspirations. Yet, we now have the good fortune to possess all of these.

To have the precious human body means to be free from the eight unfree states. These eight states are: to be born as a hell being, a hungry ghost, an animal, a long-living god, or barbarian, to have wrong views, to be born in a time without buddhas, or to be physically and mentally impaired.

However, we need something more than merely being free of the eight unfree states. We need the ten riches. There are five riches from ourselves and five riches from others. The riches from ourselves include: that we are born as a human, in a central country where there is Dharma, that we have all our senses and faculties intact, that we do not have a perverted livelihood, and that we have faith in the right objects. The riches from others are: that the Buddha appeared, he taught the Dharma, the Dharma survived, the teachings are followed by pure practitioners, and that there is someone who is willing to nurture a spiritual practitioner— a teacher. When all of these come together, then you can say, "I have obtained the precious human body."

The point of contemplating the freedoms and riches is to sincerely think about and appreciate them, so that we will decide not to waste this rare and precious opportunity. Everything else that we can achieve is nothing more than a magical illusion, a dream. Honestly, only liberation and enlightenment make sense.

Next, you contemplate how difficult it is to obtain the freedoms and riches in terms of numbers. For example, the hell beings are as numerous as atoms in the universe. The hungry ghosts are equal to the number of snowflakes in a blizzard. Animals are as numerous as yeast flakes. When we make *chang* or Tibetan beer, we use an untold number of yeast flakes. Animals and human beings are both seen on the surface of the earth. Compared to these, beings in the higher realms are as rare as the dust motes resting on the top of your thumbnail. In terms of numbers, beings with the fully endowed precious human body are very few.

Subsequently, we contemplate the precious freedoms and riches through analogy. Jamgön Kongtrül suggests using the traditional analogy of the blind turtle. Imagine a planet completely covered in water with turbulent waves. Tossed hither and thither by the waves is a wooden ring; while under the water is a blind turtle that only surfaces once every hundred years. What are the odds that it will stick its neck through the ring floating on the surface? The turtle is blind, the surface is turbulent, there is only one ring, and the turtle comes up only once every hundred years. It is next to impossible. Those are the odds we face to be reborn as a human in a precious human body.

To be reborn in this precious human body is like having found a wish-fulfilling jewel. If you desire worldly success, pleasure and comfort, it can be obtained by means of this human body. If you want to attain liberation from samsara, that also can be achieved by means of this human body. If you aim at the highest enlightenment, buddhahood, it too can be achieved by means of this human body. This body is thus extremely valuable, and having it is something to rejoice in and take advantage of. There is no sense in leaning back and thinking, "Well, if I don't make it this time, I can try in my next life." Like the blind turtle coming up for air, there is no guarantee whatsoever that you will continue in the next life as a human with all the sense faculties, good conditions, and so forth that you enjoy in the present. It is much better to make up your mind once and for all to really use this opportunity to take full advantage while you have it. Otherwise, it is as Shantideva says: "If, after having attained the freedoms and riches, you let them go to waste, there is no greater waste than that. There is nothing more foolish."

Impermanence

Next, contemplate impermanence. "Death is inevitable and I too am going to die. There is no avoiding it, and I do not have much time left." That is the contemplation.

The Buddha said, "Virtuous ones, all composite things are impermanent." Everything that is composite perishes; there are no exceptions. Everything is impermanent. Specifically, our life force is no more durable than a bubble. Certainly we understand that it is uncertain when a bubble will burst, but it will. Similarly, our human body will definitely die. Nobody has ever escaped death—not a single person. Since the body is something composite, it is sure to perish. Life never lingers for a single moment. Everything constantly changes. With each passing second, we come closer to death. As the Buddha said in a sutra, with each step you take, you draw closer to death, just like a condemned convict led to the scaffold. We should reflect carefully upon these images.

We are definitely going to die, but exactly when we will die is unknown. There is no such thing as a fixed lifespan. At any time, we can perish. Many people die at birth. Others are born with physical defects from which they quickly die. Nothing is certain. There are also accidents, diseases and various other dangers—falling off a cliff, floods, fires, wild animals, sicknesses and epidemics, evil influences, the wrong kinds of drugs and medicine, poisonous food, and so forth. In sum, how long you will live is completely uncertain. As Nagarjuna says, "The circumstances for death are numerous, and those conducive to life are few." Therefore, please practice the Dharma constantly.

Another reflection involves pondering the inevitability of the moment of death while asking what will be useful at that time. The real answer is that nothing except for our Dharma practice will truly assist us. When we die, what will become of our body and possessions? No matter how much we own, we cannot take along even a single needle. There is not a single friend, family or employee who can accompany us, regardless of how many we have. Our body too will be left behind, just thrown away. The only thing that accompanies our mind is its own good and evil, virtue and nonvirtue. Seriously, consider this. As it is said, "Apart from good and evil, nothing else accompanies a sentient being when they die. Ponder this fact carefully and make the right choice."

Jamgön Kongtrül concludes this reflection by saying, "This being so, I realize that nothing else whatsoever can help me at the time of death, nor after death, in all my lifetimes. The sacred Dharma is the one true benefit, and nothing else. Therefore, from this day onwards, I will apply myself wholeheartedly to practicing the sublime teachings." That is the whole purpose of this reflection: to resolve to practice the Dharma as much as we can from this very day onwards.

Suffering

Next comes the reflection on the suffering of the lower realms. We are going to die—that much is certain—but it does not end there. We will take another rebirth, and we do not have a direct choice as to where we will be reborn. Our own positive or negative actions will propel us into the higher or lower realms.

Lifespans in the hell realms are extremely long, much longer than those of human beings. There is no escape from the various torments there. In the highest of the hell realms, corpses blaze on fire. In some places, you fall into a swamp of putrid water or molten metal. In the liquid are small animals that gnaw at your flesh and peel it off, piece by piece, while the rest of the body continues to burn. Then there are vicious beings that push you back down anytime you are able to get your head above the surface. Countless horrible animals like snakes and malicious carnivores roam about, and every time you recover your senses, they kill you again. This is only the highest of the hell realms. Each lower level gets worse, all the way down to the hell called the 'hell of incessant torment,' which is the eighth hot hell. The suffering there is unbearable.

There are also eight cold hells where you freeze—the skin blisters and becomes covered in open sores, from which pus flows. The body decays like a withered lotus blossom, falling to pieces. Each cold hell is successively more freezing. There are further torments in each of the four directions: the pit of fiery embers, the swamp of rotten corpses, the path filled with swords and the forest of blades. These are temporary hells in which you suffer for a time, and then obtain some relief before being tormented again. Clearly, the beings in the hell realms go through endless suffering. Reflect on each of these realms and the types of suffering they entail.

Next is the reflection on what it is like to be a hungry ghost. Some hungry ghosts live underground in the realm of Yama, while others live on the surface of the earth, flying around. In the sutra called *The Application of Mindfulness*, the Buddha mentions thirty-six kinds of hungry ghosts. I will discuss three of them. There are those with the external obscuration, who always see food and drink as rotten, poisoned or filthy, so that they are unable to enjoy it. They may see water in the distance, but when they approach, they discover it has dried up. They may see fruit hanging on a tree, but it is guarded so that they are prevented from picking any. The essence of their state is that they have no chance to enjoy anything. They constantly yearn; yet never obtain what they long for.

Hungry ghosts with the inner obscuration are those who are unable to enjoy food and drink. In *A Letter to a Friend,* Nagarjuna says that they feel as if they have a mouth as tiny as the eye of a needle, and a belly as big as a valley. Even if they manage to get a tiny scrap of food down their throats, it does not help because they are so immensely hungry. Everything feels dirty and filthy, and they have no chance to ever feel fulfilled.

The third type of hungry ghost has the obscuration for food and drink. Whatever they eat immediately turns into fire that burns their belly. Some cannot eat any normal food; they can only eat shit and drink piss. They are constantly hungry and thirsty, always searching, tired and exhausted. They have no clothes, and they feel burnt, starving, poor, stressed and suffering with intense anguish. The average lifespan of a hungry ghost is fifteen thousand years.

When pondering what it is like to be an animal, think of the creatures who live in the oceans' depths and those who live on land. In the depths of the ocean, there is no fixed home for anybody. Beings there do not live in any specific place, but are constantly moved around by the currents. There is no certainty as to where they will be. They eat each other continuously. The larger ones eat the smaller ones, and the smaller eat the even smaller ones. They constantly suffer from fear and anxiety as to what is going to happen next. There is no being at ease anywhere for a creature in the ocean.

Animals who live on land are either wild or domesticated. A wild animal is always being hunted. There is no security anywhere. There is always the fear that somebody is going to swoop down and eat you. Domesticated animals are used for riding or carrying loads, or are raised and then killed for their skin or their flesh. They experience unbelievable suffering, and the only choice is to try to endure it. Their suffering is truly unbearable, but they cannot talk and express their pain; nor can they escape into a different situation.

When we think about this situation with utter honesty, are we certain that we will not be born into one of those states, either as a hell being, a hungry ghost, or an animal? Actually, we do not truly possess the confidence that we can avoid these sorts of rebirths. There is no real assurance that it will not happen to us. Whoever is reborn in these realms will undergo these sufferings—there is no way around it. Thinking of this, there seems to be only one choice: a firm decision that I will really practice the true Dharma from now on.

The Consequences of Karma

The next reflection is about the consequences of our actions. In *The Sutra of One Hundred Karmas,* the Buddha explains that karma is the myriad sorts of actions that create countless types of sentient beings. Karmic actions and their effects are very difficult to specifically define. It is a very open-ended topic.

Karma can take form in all sorts of ways. Any state that is comfortable or uncomfortable, easy or uneasy, results from nothing other than the previous creation of negative or positive karma. The result of virtuous action is to experience pleasure and comfort. The result of negative action is to experience pain or anxiety. Karma is like seeds planted in a field: whichever seed is sown is the one that will ripen. When we do something good or evil, it may look very small or insignificant, but slowly this can change so that its effect can multiply hundreds or thousands of times. Therefore, the result of any particular action can be extremely significant.

Another point is that karma does not disappear. Once something is done, whether it is good or evil, small or big, it will always ripen, unless an antidote eliminates it. It does not vanish even with the passing of time. An additional aspect of karma is that we do not meet any circumstance devoid of previous karmic connection. Furthermore, only we experience the ripening of our self-produced karma. No one else will. The Buddha has said, "You do not meet with something you have not created, and whatever you do never vanishes. Be careful about what you accept or reject." When we think about this, we want to be more careful about avoiding negative actions and adopting positive ones.

There are ten main negative actions to consider. The first is taking the life of another, either through desire, anger or stupidity. It could be a sentient being of either higher or lesser importance. Second is to take what is not given. This can occur through force, as in robbery, or through deception, as in stealing by a thief. If a business profit is gained through trickery, the business falls in the category of deceit. The third negative action is sexual misconduct, which includes having contact with someone who is committed to another person or who is under the guardianship of the Dharma. These are the three negative karmic actions through our body.

After that are the four negative karmic actions through our speech. These are: to lie, which means telling what is not true; to engage in divisive talk either directly, indirectly or in a concealed way and to speak harsh words, either directly, indirectly or implicitly. Finally, there is idle gossip, which is either completely wrong, mundane or very pointless.

The three negative karmic actions occurring through our mind are to covet something for oneself, for others or for both, and to harbor ill will out of hatred, jealousy or resentment. Lastly, there is the holding of wrong views about karma, about the truth, and about the Three Jewels. Together these are called the ten unvirtuous actions. Each of them generates a specific ripening of karma corresponding to the cause. Actions that have an effect that accords with the opposite of these are the ten virtuous actions.

When we do these ten unvirtuous actions motivated primarily by hatred, if we repeat them many times, or commit them towards a loved one or a sublime being, the result is our rebirth as a hell being. If they are done out of desire, in a medium amount, or towards a middling object, the result is rebirth as a hungry ghost. If done out of stupidity or in a lesser amount, the result will be rebirth as an animal. Since it is true that these actions cause the sufferings of the lower realms, please make up your minds to apply methods that purify them. Henceforth take the vow to not commit them again with firm determination.

The opposite of the ten unvirtuous actions is to engage in the ten virtuous actions that bring forth positive results. Not only do we give up the ten negative actions; in addition, we engage in virtue. We save lives and are generous and decent in our conduct. We speak truthfully, gently, kindly and meaningfully. We reconcile enmity and have less craving. By means of these behaviors, we develop contentment, generate more benevolence, have trust in the consequences of actions, and develop the threefold trust in the Three Jewels.

We will take rebirth in our future lives in accordance with the strength, the degree and the number of our virtuous actions. In the higher instances, we will be born as a god, in the lesser ones, as a human being. If good and evil are mixed together, we will take birth as a demigod. The reason for thinking about this now is to form the clear realization that these ten virtuous actions are the cause of all happiness and wellbeing. We should firmly resolve to always keep them in mind, and to cultivate and perform them as much as possible.

I mentioned earlier that the first stepping stones for the path is trust and renunciation. These four reflections, known as the four mind-changings, have a definite purpose. They are not merely for us to think and feel bad about. Their real intention is to help us develop renunciation, which comes about naturally when we think about these four reflections. True renunciation means we have the will to be free of the samsaric state. Renunciation does not come naturally without any effort. That is why it is necessary to spend time on these reflections. If you ponder these reflections repeatedly and actually take them to heart, thinking, "What would it be like in the lower realms?" you will eventually truly wish to be free. That is the purpose here.

This completes the teachings on the four reflections.

Refuge

To develop trust and devotion, in addition to the four mind-changings, there is the instruction on taking refuge. To be rescued from taking further rebirth in the three lower realms and enduring unbearable suffering, we must take refuge in someone who has the capacity to liberate us. We cannot be liberated by ourselves. Sentient beings do not have the ability to pull themselves out of the three lower realms. Moreover, it does not help to seek support from mundane individuals or even gods such as Brahma, Indra or the like. As mentioned in *The Great Nirvana Sutra*, "By taking refuge in the Three Jewels, you will attain a state beyond fear," meaning fear of the lower realms. These are the reasons we go for refuge in the Three Jewels.

First, develop and maintain a vivid sense of the presence of the representations of enlightened body, speech and mind. Remember that what we regard as being in front of ourselves is merely a support. What we actually take refuge in are the qualities of realization. In this sense, the Three Jewels are embodied in the precious Buddha who represents the dharmakaya, sambhogakaya, and nirmanakaya, the identity that embodies all three kayas. The sacred Dharma is the Dharma of both statements and of realization. The noble Sangha are those endowed with that realization. That is the real meaning of the Three Jewels. Moreover, we regard the Buddha as the teacher, the Dharma as the path, and the Sangha as our companions on the path. The ultimate object of refuge is the Buddha's completely realized state of being. In the *Uttaratantra Shastra* it is written, "The true meaning of taking refuge is exclusively the Buddha," meaning the awakened state.

In this particular context, Arya Tara embodies all objects of refuge. In other words, all the victorious ones—all buddhas and bodhisattvas—are included within the single form of Arya Tara, who is actually *Prajñaparamita* in person. Her form is the Sangha, her speech is the sacred Dharma, and her mind is the nature of the Buddha, the awakened state.

Imagine that Tara is in the sky before you, seated upon a lotus flower resting atop a moon disc. Take refuge in her as being indivisible from your own root guru. Imagine that she is surrounded by all Three Jewels, all those who are able to bestow refuge. Her right hand is raised in the gesture of bestowing protection. You sit beneath that, along with all other sentient beings who need protection and refuge.[18] Her blessings protect you from your fears of samsara, especially of taking rebirth in the lower realms. Confident that you are thus forever protected, and with one-pointed devotion, repeat the verse for taking refuge:

NAMO
In the guru, the yidam, Arya Tara,
The Three Jewels and the ocean of conquerors,
With one-pointed devotion, I and all sentient beings
Take refuge until enlightenment.

Repeat this one hundred, a thousand, or ten thousand times, or whatever set number you have decided to do.

After having repeated a set number of recitations of the refuge verse, imagine that the object of refuge—in other words Tara—melts into light. Absorbing her, blessings enter your stream of being. Then simply let go of any focus and settle in the state of equanimity free of mental constructs.

After a while, dedicate the merit. This is the general way of practicing during a session of taking refuge.

The general taking of refuge also includes what to avoid and what to adopt. For example, having taken refuge in the Buddha, we avoid turning to non-Buddhist teachings for support. Having taken refuge in the Dharma, we avoid harming sentient beings. Having taken refuge in the Sangha, we avoid company with non-Buddhists and extremist teachers. The three things to adopt involve respecting even the minutest representations of the Buddha, Dharma and Sangha. Always pay respect to even a tiny statue, a single page of scripture, or a small fragment of a Dharma robe. The subsidiary training is to offer the first part of our food to the Three Jewels, to bow down to the Three Jewels before traveling anywhere, and to encourage ourselves and others to place trust in the Buddha, Dharma and Sangha.

In this way, we follow the general training of being a Buddhist. Special benefits accrue from doing so, such as the fact that negative karma will gradually diminish and be purified. Taking refuge forms the support for the advanced practices, so that we gradually proceed towards a higher and higher level of realization, and finally attain enlightenment and buddhahood.

With these four reflections and the taking of refuge, we have covered the practices for those of the most basic capacity, the elemental type of person.

For Those of Medium Capacity

This second section is on the training in the steps of the teaching for those of medium capacity. It has two parts;

namely, reflecting upon the causes of both samsara and liberation.

Samsara

The reflection on samsara also has two parts: considering both the result, which is suffering, as well as the origin of this suffering.

For the former, Jamgön Kongtrül instructs us to think as follows: "If I succeed in escaping the three lower realms, will being born in the higher realms suffice? It is definitely not perfect happiness, because if I am born again as a human, the eight types of suffering will torment me, starting with the suffering of being born. While in my mother's womb, I am constricted. It is dark and filthy, and I am constantly uncomfortable. When my mother has filled her belly, it seems like a mountain is crushing me. When her belly is empty, it feels as if I am dangling over a precipice. When her food and drink are too hot or too cold, I suffer. When I am born, it feels like being squeezed through the eye of a needle or the hole in an anvil. After birth, even when I am wrapped in the softest cloth, it feels as if I have been tossed into a nest of thorns. When somebody picks me up, it feels as if a hawk is holding me with its talons."

This is how a sensitive baby experiences everything at the beginning. These sensations are almost unbearable. Continue by thinking, "This is what I will experience upon being born. This is what birth feels like. And each of these painful sensations is the seed for further suffering, resulting in old age, sickness, and death. Upon meeting these circumstances, further emotional states will be triggered. Birth is the basis for all negative emotions that arise. All that birth brings is the unending experience of being propelled from one painful state to another."

We can continue as follows: "Next, when I start to age, there are also five types of suffering. The first is that my luster diminishes and my flesh loses its color. My skin becomes grimy; my hair grows white, and so on. The second is that I lose my shape; my teeth fall out; my back becomes bent; my arms and legs become crooked; and my flesh and skin wither. My strength will wane until I cannot easily stand up, and yet it feels uncomfortable to sit for a long time. My senses will weaken—my eyesight will go, as will my hearing. Eventually, I will lose my ability to enjoy anything. When there is not enough food, I feel constantly hungry. If I get too much, I cannot digest it, and so forth." Those five types of discomfort accompany aging.

Then there is the pain of sickness. "When falling sick, there is pain and anguish. The muscle tissue deteriorates; the skin dries up; the constitution of the body degenerates. When I am ill, I lack the ability to enjoy anything, even pleasant things. I have to undergo painful medical procedures. There is even the anguish caused by the fear of losing my life.

"When death finally does come, I will need to part from my possessions, friends, family, attendants, employees, and everything that brings me pleasure. My very body will be left behind, and I will experience intense dread and anxiety. Moreover, I will also experience worry at being unable to keep what I have: property, fame, good name, food, wealth, horses, cattle, etc. Even when I have possessions, I must constantly toil first to accumulate, and then guard them. Day and night, I am plagued by many worries. When the slightest loss occurs, there is an intense anguish. The suffering of trying to achieve and find what I do not possess—wealth, food, property—requires constant laborious effort. Even at the cost of being hungry and thirsty, I still need to carry on. Even at the cost of life and limb, I need to exert myself.

"Moreover, there is the suffering of meeting with the unwanted—with enemies, with someone resentful or desiring revenge, with bandits, thieves, wild animals, and the like. When any of these suddenly appear, or when I am a subject of a capricious local ruler, or when the servants of the rich misbehave, all kinds of painful unwanted events can take place.

"Furthermore, there is the suffering of being parted from those I love: my father and mother, my siblings, my spouse, children, friends, followers. I fear the time when I must helplessly depart and leave behind my property and possessions. They will disappear; my money and articles could be destroyed. My cattle and horses may die, or there might come a plague. When any of these happen to someone that I am attached to, I experience deepfelt sorrow." All of these sufferings belong to the anguish of being a human.

We can go on: "If I am born as an asura, a demigod, then from the very moment I take that form I experience an intense sense of competitiveness and rivalry that makes me want to compete and fight, especially against the devas." Since asuras have less merit, they always lose in the battle against the gods, inevitably being beaten or killed. Asuras have a negative attitude in that they lack trust and interest in Dharma practice.

"If I am born as one of the gods, I am continually distracted by my comforts. Because my lifespan is so long, I have no impetus to practice the Dharma. When the end of my long life is near, it does not feel like it's been any more than a fleeting moment. Noticing the omens of impending death, my despair is intense. I don't feel I can rest or sit anywhere. The garlands of flowers look old; my garments look soiled and smell bad; my skin is sweaty. My godly friends and companions begin to flee; they do not want to stay around. After passing to the next life, I will discover that rebirth in the realms below cannot be avoided, and this fact is intensely painful, almost unendurable. In short, no matter what state in samsara that I may be reborn in, there is no place that has any real happiness."

As Guru Rinpoche says, "In this samsara, which is like sitting on the tip of a needle, there is never any real pleasure. Even when there is a minor comfort, it always changes." Every type of neutral sensation experienced by the mind and body—the 'five perpetuating aggregates'—is also painful, as they are permeated by being conditioned. All samsaric states, without a single exception, are infused with the nature of suffering. In the three lower realms, there is disease and infinite types of evil influences. Even in the higher realms there are numerous agonizing sensations, painful in that they cause suffering.

Even in the samadhi states belonging to the *dhyana* states in the Form Realms and Formless Realms, the highest samadhis, the pleasure and joys are also painful in that they change. In other words, the suffering of change permeates pleasant sensations, and all sensations as a whole. Therefore, "I shall develop the intention to attain liberation, to be free. Within samsara, whether I am in a higher or lower state, whether there is pleasure or pain, whether there are enemies or friends, whether I have parent or child, the place, the body, the enjoyments, and so forth—are all uncertain. There is no predictability anywhere. Whatever the joy and whatever the objects of enjoyment that I might experience, they are never truly fulfilling. Any suffering I experience is invariably depressing, yet I am not fed up. I need to shed the body every time I am reborn, only to repeatedly take birth again and again. Every type of joy or sorrow, success or failure, from high or low, I must undergo alone. There is no friend, no helper in birth, old age, sickness, and death in all this suffering that I endure."

To sum up, samsara is characterized by an amazing amount of ordeals. It is similar to being thrown again and again into a pit of burning embers, or to being on death row. When you start to see everything like this, you will genuinely engender the thought, 'I must be free!'

The Origin of Suffering

The last section dealt with reflecting on the results of samsaric existence and coming to the conclusion that samsaric states are painful. Next, we reflect on the cause of samsara, the very origin of suffering. The painful states of samsara do not happen without reasons. They are simply the inevitable consequence of karmic actions, which themselves result from negative emotions. These emotions are classified as the six primary types or the nine fetters, which include the 84,000 different mental events. Six, nine, or 84,000—all of them can be included within the three root poisons. The three root poisons themselves are embedded in the ignorance of failing to realize the natural state.

All obscurations, including clinging to the five aggregates and the concept of a solid ego, unfold from that basic obscuration of failing to realize the natural state. Holding that self to be truly existing, dear and important is one of the primary causes of samsaric existence. Harmful views result from this self-cherishing. Attachment to your body, mind, feelings, possessions and the particular sentient beings who are close to you produces conceit, jealousy and stinginess. Whenever there is an expectation of harm or threat towards "me," "my side," or "my people," aggression and hatred arise. The outward expression of such an attitude is hostility, fury and spite. All of these emotions create unmeritorious karmic actions that result in rebirth in the lower realms of samsara.

The effect of meritorious actions is rebirth in the higher realms. There is also a type called 'nontransferring actions' that result in the conditioned meditative states of the dhyana states of the form realms and formless realms. All beings are tossed about within samsaric states due to causes that are the origin of samsara, the emotions. By all means, free yourself from these. That is the attitude that you should harbor. Repeatedly examine your own mind to see whether the emotional states that create samsara are present.

Liberation

We have now covered the causes and effects within samsara. Next comes the cause and effect of liberation. On this point, Jamgön Kongtrül asks you to reflect as follows: "I want to eliminate the causes for samsaric existence, and I aim to be completely free. The cause for liberation is unconditioned insight, the true realization of the natural state that is free of ego-clinging, which has the capacity to eliminate all negative emotional states. This is what I want to pursue. The cause of this true insight is one-pointed samadhi. Therefore, I need the cause of samadhi, which is the utterly pure discipline of renunciation. Thus, right now, in order to free myself from samsara, I will stick to the discipline, train in samadhi, and generate true insight in the sense of understanding the meaning of impermanence, suffering, emptiness and egolessness." This is the intention we should form.

It is the combination of all of the above topics that serves as the preliminary instruction for the practice of the person of medium capacity. In other words, we want to be free of samsara, of all samsaric states, the causes of which are the three poisons of ignorance, attachment and aggression. We must eliminate the causes. The way to eliminate the cause of ignorance and ego-clinging is true insight into the meaning of impermanence, suffering, emptiness and egolessness. For that to happen, we need to have one-pointed concentration, which is samadhi. However, in order to have one-pointedness of mind, renunciation of samsaric states is necessary. This is why discipline, samadhi and superior insight are necessary. Having understood this, the training here is to form the decision to develop these three qualities.

The Excellence of the Middle — Mahayana

Now comes the explanation for the second section, the excellence of the middle, which is connected to the Mahayana and the practice for the superior type of person, namely, the noble intention. This path has two aspects. First is the entrance door, which is training in the intent; second is how to expand and apply that.

To train in the noble intention you must develop a certain attitude. I have already explained how it is necessary to eliminate the causes and the sufferings of samsara and attain liberation and nirvana. It is possible to attain liberation either as a shravaka or pratyekabuddha, but there is another way, which is buddhahood. A buddha has perfect, complete realization, has abandoned any selfish interest in personal benefit, and manifests unconditioned activity that benefits others. The true and complete enlightenment of the buddha is what we must attain. The training itself is in developing this noble intent. Incessantly cultivate the strong wish to attain enlightenment.

Having formed the intention to benefit others, we must expand it. This training has two aspects—reflecting on the relationship between cause and effect, and reflecting on the meaning. The relationship between cause and effect is as Kongtrül writes: "I want to attain buddhahood, complete enlightenment. If that is going to happen, I must have the cause for buddhahood, which is bodhichitta. The cause of bodhichitta is compassion. The root of compassion is loving kindness, so therefore I must develop loving kindness. To develop loving kindness, I must acknowledge and wish to repay the kindness of others. I want to repay this kindness because I understand that every single sentient being in samsara has been my parent. In other words, all the infinite number of beings throughout space are my parents. Every one of them has been kind to me, and every one of them wants to be free of suffering. How wonderful if they could be free of suffering and have happiness! To establish them all in happiness, I must become a buddha. Even if I attain buddhahood, I must still bring everyone else to buddhahood as well."

Loving Kindness

First comes loving kindness, second, compassion and finally, training in bodhichitta. To develop loving kindness, you can imagine your own mother right in front of you. Then bring to mind that, "My own kind mother produced this body that I now have, an effort which caused her a lot of hardship and trouble. She has given me this precious life, taken care of me, and performed every single action necessary for me to survive in this world. She regarded me with a love greater than she had for her own self. She protected me. She gave me all the help and support I needed to grow up. When threatened by harm, she protected me, which is a great kindness. Wouldn't it be amazing if my mother could be happy and truly at ease? And it is not just my present mother—in all my countless other lives, I have had mothers who have done exactly the same, loving mothers who have bestowed upon me similar help and love. This happened not only once, as a parent, but also as a friend, a lover, and a companion. All these people have helped me in all kinds of ways. Thinking of my own mother who is very dear to me and helped me, I now want to return her kindness." Loving kindness should thus be engendered in our hearts until it becomes a distinct and very clearly manifested feeling.

Having generated this loving kindness to your own mother, extend it to include other family members and friends, people in your neighborhood, in your country, and so on, until gradually you've included all the sentient beings in the billionfold universes. Embrace all the six classes of sentient beings with the same loving kindness you generate for your present mother. This is the second aspect.

Next try to engender this intention: "Just as all these sentient beings have been my own mothers, may they all be happy and at ease. Moreover, may I be able to bring them contentment and ease in a flawless way. May I be able to establish them in perfect happiness."

There is a quote in *The Jewel Garland*, *The Ratnavali,* about the benefits of training in loving kindness—that compared to being generous with food in a myriad of ways; one moment of loving kindness has much greater merit. The key point here is to start by imagining your own mother and what she did for you, then expand it until it includes all sentient beings.

Compassion

Next is training in compassion. Just as we reflected on our kind mother, we should then think, "All sentient beings are my own mothers and wish to have happiness and wellbeing. Yet, they experience nothing but misery and suffering. In the three lower realms they experience the suffering resulting from their past actions, while in the higher realms they create the causes for further suffering. If they produce severe negative karma while in the higher realms, at the moment of death, they will immediately fall into the state of a hell being. There is no escape. It is almost unbearable to think of my own mother falling into the state of a hell being." Imagine over and over that your own mother takes rebirth in hell—first your present mother, then expanding from her to encompass all beings. Imagine how she is going to be consumed in the blazing flames, and how she will be frozen in the cold hells until totally petrified. Imagine how she will be tortured or chopped into pieces in the other hell realms, her arms and legs amputated, and so on. Thinking in this way will generate extreme compassion. Then think, "This is how all sentient beings in those places suffer, and they were all my own mothers."

Similarly, how would my mother feel if she was hungry or starved and tormented by disease in the hungry ghost realm? What would it be like for her if she were imprisoned, chained, beaten, enslaved, and abused by others as an animal? What if she were blind and standing at the edge of a very steep cliff, not knowing how to proceed without falling? She does not know what to do or how to proceed, and is about to fall into the abyss. The moment she falls, there is no escape from suffering.

That is how we train, by repeatedly imagining these various scenarios in order to develop an almost unbearable feeling of compassion. We then extend this sense of compassion from one person to many, just as we did with loving kindness. This is how we expand the compassion to become more sincere and genuine, until we start to feel a very sincere intention. We think, "My mothers, all the sentient beings of the six classes—May I protect all of them from negative karma and from suffering! May I lead all of them out of samsara's painful states! May I separate all of them from suffering and from the causes of suffering, the negative emotions!"

We train repeatedly like this, till we come to the point where we have that intention always in the forefront of our minds. The text *In Praise of Avalokiteshvara* states, "If you possess a single quality that is equal to having every teaching of the buddhas in the palm of your hand, it is great compassion." This hints at the inconceivable benefits of developing compassion.

First, check how compassionate you actually are and how much loving kindness you truly have. Realizing that it is not very much, try to generate more. When you do feel some loving kindness and compassion, increase it further and further. That is something to focus on. Train in giving up selfishness and being concerned only with yourself. Instead of primarily concentrating on your own needs and interests, practice exchanging yourself with others.

Begin by regarding yourself and others as being equal. Next, exchange yourself with others, so that they are more important than you. The way to do that is by sending out your pleasure or happiness and taking in their pain or sorrow. In other words, do the tonglen practice of exchanging your own happiness with the suffering of others. As Shantideva said, "Unless you fully take the suffering of others upon yourself, you will not obtain enlightenment; and there is no happiness in samsara." If you cannot put yourself in another's place, there is no way to attain enlightenment.

Jamgön Kongtrül explains how to train in this practice. We begin by thinking, "I want to be happy, and I don't want to suffer. Every other sentient being has the exact same wish. We are all equal in that sense. I am merely one among infinite numbers of sentient beings. Even though we are equal in the sense of desiring happiness, they should be more important, since there are so many more of them. As they are all my own mothers, I will take upon myself any suffering that they do not want. I should give my own mothers the happiness that they wish for."

Combine this with your breath as follows: when you exhale, generate the attitude that thinks, "Whatever virtue, good karma, pleasure, and happiness I have created from beginningless time until now, I completely exhale and send to all sentient beings. In both body and mind may they have peace and wellbeing." Have full confidence that they receive it. While inhaling, imagine that whatever they have created since beginningless lifetimes, all the causes for suffering— karma, negative emotions, evil actions, obscurations, and so forth—as well as the resultant suffering, is completely absorbed into you and dissolves, leaving all beings completely free from both the causes and results of suffering. Having that kind of confidence, perform this inhalation and exhalation. You do this so that all sentient beings may have happiness and so that all their suffering may ripen upon yourself. To train in this sincerely is the mind-training for compassion.

BODHICHITTA OF ASPIRATION

Next comes the training in the aspiring resolve. For the bodhichitta of aspiration, we train as Jamgön Kongtrül states, in this thought: "May my parents, all sentient beings, constantly have wellbeing. May they be perpetually free of suffering. In addition, may they attain complete buddhahood. In order for that to happen, I must first, for their sake, attain the state of a true and completely awakened one. Upon attaining buddhahood, I will lead every sentient being without exception out of samsara's ocean of suffering and establish them in the state of the Buddha." That kind of resolve is called aspiring towards enlightenment.

Simply forming the aspiring resolve, the bodhichitta of aspiration, will ultimately accomplish the welfare of both self and others. It eliminates all personal flaws and produces all the virtuous qualities. The benefits of this are inconceivable. They are mentioned in *The Sutra Requested by Resplendent Generosity:* "If the merit of bodhichitta were to have physical form, it would fill the entirety of space and be even larger."

Having formed this aspiring resolve, it is necessary to actually train in it. The way to do this is to never give up the wish to help other beings. Adopt the four positive qualities and give up their opposites. Day and night, work at increasing the two accumulations of merit and wisdom.

Let me explain the statement "to never give up the wish to help other beings," a little more deeply. Once you have entered the Mahayana path, never forsake any sentient beings. Never think that you cannot attain enlightenment. To do so could cause you to give up the Mahayana, the teachings of the Greater Vehicle. Then you will become completely self-absorbed, reverting to doing things exclusively for yourself. Doing this is the same as rejecting the primary cause for attaining buddhahood. The repercussions are obviously extremely harmful. Moreover, do not form the angry thought toward any sentient being, "May I never meet you again," or, "May I never help you." Finally do not ever beat, hurt or even have the wish to harm an animal, a thief or a living creature even as small as a louse. Any action like this is called forsaking the benefit of sentient beings.

The four negative characteristics are, first, to deceive a venerable person, a master or somebody worthy of respect—a receptacle of offerings. It is extremely bad to deceive such a person by lies or any kind of dishonesty. The second is to cause someone to regret that which is not to be regretted. For example, to commit an evil action is a cause of regret, while performing a positive action is not. The third negative characteristic is to disparage a person who has generated bodhichitta. Do not utter even one word that directly or indirectly defames or criticizes a bodhisattva. The fourth one is to deceive a sentient being, either by manipulation or by direct lies for selfish purposes. Do not play misleading tricks on people—do not even fool with weights and scales in business. All of these have very negative repercussions.

To turn away from these and train in their opposites is called the four virtuous qualities. That means, first, to be truthful and avoid deceiving others, even at the cost of your life. Try to establish all beings in your merit, and especially in the bodhichitta resolve. Persevere in advancing them in the virtuous roots of the Greater Vehicle. Regard whoever has developed bodhichitta as the real teacher, as a buddha, and always praise their qualities. Never deceive another sentient being. Always take upon yourself the burden of benefiting others with noble intentions. Also, to the best of your abilities, engage in creating the accumulation of merit through thoughts, words, and deeds. Devote yourself towards study, reflection and meditation practice, and the teachings of the true accumulation of wisdom. These are the trainings in the bodhichitta of aspiration that we should undertake.

Bodhichitta of Application

After the aspiring resolve comes the applied resolve—the bodhichitta of application—that has two aspects: the general and specific trainings. It is not enough to merely wish to attain complete enlightenment. We need to train in the activities that are causes for this attainment. These activities are vast and extensive, but their very essence is the six paramitas and the four means of magnetizing. Make the conscious decision that through these, "I will embark upon the activities of a bodhisattva in order to attain enlightenment for the sake of all beings."

Next, resolve to abide by the four means of magnetizing. These are described in a scripture entitled *The Lotus Mound:* "Agreeably beckon sentient beings with the fan of generosity, welcome them with pleasantly spoken words, make them feel at ease with meaningful action, and give them consistent advice." In brief, teaching others by using words and applying what you have said causes them to embrace the teachings. Those four lines contain both the six paramitas as well as the four means of magnetizing. In sum, one vows to consistently practice the six paramitas, not at some point in the future, but from this very moment. That is a very important decision to take.

Now, here is how to make the bodhisattva resolve. First, you take the vow in the presence of a master or in front of a sacred object. On a daily basis, make the pledge either three times or accumulate a set number all the way up to one hundred thousand. To do this, imagine that Arya Tara, vividly present and alive as if in person, is in the sky before you, surrounded by all the buddhas and bodhisattvas.

With them as witness, form the pledge to attain complete enlightenment. Then for the sake of all beings, you take the vow as a wish, and as something you actually put into practice. Keeping this in mind, you repeat the following verse,

> HO,
> In order to ensure that all sentient beings, my mothers,
> Attain the state of enlightenment,
> I will refrain from misdeeds, gather all virtuous
>   qualities,
> And always generate the bodhichitta that benefits
>   others.

Repeat this verse however many times is suitable. At the end of the session, totally dispense with any mental constructs of objective enlightenment, an actual person forming the bodhisattva vow and the act of doing so. Settle then into the state of equanimity. This is called "sealing relative bodhichitta with ultimate bodhichitta." In other words, simply remain in the ultimate state of bodhichitta. Finish the session by dedicating the merit.

Within this training in the bodhichitta of application, once we have formed the resolve to actually apply the path to enlightenment, there are certain trainings that we must go through. These can be condensed into 'three superior trainings' described in Atisha's *Lamp for the Path to Enlightenment*: "If you want to summarize the nature of the applied resolve, it is to dedicate yourself thoroughly to the training of discipline, samadhi and insight, with great devotion in these three trainings."

The training in discipline includes the paramitas of generosity, discipline and patience. The training in samadhi is comprised of the fifth paramita, concentration, while the training in insight is the sixth paramita, the transcendent knowledge. The fourth paramita of perseverance supports all three trainings. *The Ornament of the Sutras* says, "The conquerors have clearly taught that the three trainings are the six paramitas. The first three comprise the first training, the last two have one each, and the fourth belongs to all three of them."

The six paramitas encompass every single activity necessary for attaining enlightenment. As the Buddha taught in *The Sutra Requested by Subahu*, "Subahu, a bodhisattva mahasattva who wishes to quickly attain true and complete enlightenment should, constantly and always, thoroughly embrace the six paramitas." The six paramitas are the direct cause of attaining the higher realms, liberation and enlightenment.

For the sake of gaining an exalted rebirth, be generous. For the purpose of rebirth in the higher realms, maintain the discipline of pure ethics. In order to have a retinue of followers, be patient. In order to attain the definite goodness of liberation and enlightenment, be diligent in promoting virtuous qualities. Train in concentration, which is the cause of shamatha, and train in insight (*prajña*), which is the cause of vipashyana.

To progress gradually, train in the easier paramitas first, followed by the subtler. Form the pledge: "For the sake of accomplishing buddhahood by the path of the higher realms to the definite goodness of liberation, I take it upon myself to endeavor in the six paramitas, going progressively through the easiest to the more difficult." This is the oath that we take.

The six paramitas can also be included within the two accumulations in the following way: generosity and discipline belong to the accumulation of merit, while insight is the accumulation of wisdom. The other three—patience, concentration and perseverance—encompass both accumulations. Each of the five first paramitas weakens its opposite, the adverse circumstances. They promote thoughtfree wakefulness and fulfill all aims you may have. They are endowed with the four qualities that bring benefit to sentient beings.

Now comes something very important: the first five paramitas must be embraced by the sixth paramita, an insight that does not conceptualize the three spheres. In other words, be free of concepts. Otherwise, they will not be causes for attaining enlightenment. When you do embrace each and every paramita with transcendent knowledge, they truly are a paramita, which means 'transcendent.' In this way, you will attain the state of omniscient buddhahood.

The Compendium, a Mahayana scripture, explains how "blind people need at least one guide in the beginning to show them the way. The sixth paramita is like the eye, somebody who can see, and he can lead the other ones along to the city of enlightenment. In this way, embrace the first five paramitas with transcendent knowledge. Without doing so, you will not reach the city of complete enlightenment."

Accordingly, we should now take the pledge that, "I will train myself to the best of my ability, constantly and always, in generosity and the other paramitas. Whatever I might do, I will form the right intention, next practice, and make the right conclusion. But especially I will embrace all of these with the flawless insight that does not conceptualize the three spheres. I will embrace them by the two accumulations for the benefit of all sentient beings. I will practice each paramita and training, making sure they possess these four perfect qualities. Furthermore, within the state of not conceptualizing the three spheres, I will carry out everything with the continuous understanding that all is like a magical illusion." That is the pledge we take; our training is to endeavor in that pledge.

In short, *apply* the bodhichitta of aspiration by means of the six paramitas and the four means of magnetizing.

The Six Paramitas

Unfortunately, it is not enough just to know the names of the six paramitas: we should also know what they actually mean. I will describe them specifically one by one in an explanation that has three sections. The discussion of the first four paramitas will be in brief, the last two, concentration and insight, will be given in more detail.

In training in the applied resolve, the bodhichitta of application, first is the paramita of generosity. Generosity has three aspects. The giving of material things is to give to whomever is in need food, clothing, money, material articles, necessities, or whatever else they lack. This should be done to the best of your ability, with a pure attitude and the appropriate materials. Often our giving is flawed in either motive or attitude, but it is important to give with pure intent and without clinging. The conduct and the giving must be perfect.

Next is the giving of fearlessness or removing anxiety. You do this by giving others relief from disease, poisons, toxins, warfare, weapons, wildfires, floods and attacks by vicious animals. Additionally, you help alleviate the fears of people traveling on dangerous roads and those in prison. To rescue people in cases like this is a form of generosity, relieving their apprehension and trepidation.

Lastly is the giving of truth. If you have the ability to teach the Dharma and explain the teachings so that others can attain liberation, then you should do so, but without any regard for honor, fame, or personal benefit. If you are unable to teach, you should simply read aloud the words of the buddhas, so that they can be heard by humans, spirits, and so on.

The second paramita, discipline (*shila*), also has three aspects. The first of these is the discipline of refraining from harmful deeds. In this regard, there are two kinds of wrongdoing. One is by default, which involves the ten unvirtuous actions. You could say that these are natural transgressions. But there is also the fault of going against what you have pledged. In other words, it is harmful to go against any type of vow, whether you have taken precepts of any one of the six types of *pratimoksha,* individual liberation, one of the two types of bodhichitta vows or the primary and subsidiary tantric samayas. To avoid such transgressions is the first type of discipline.

The second type of discipline is to produce virtuous qualities through effort in thought, word and deed. Whether they are small or large does not matter—simply do the best you can. Finally, there is the discipline of supporting sentient beings, to work for the welfare of others. There are many forms of superior intention, both direct and indirect, that establish you and all other sentient beings in what is virtuous and beneficial.

The third paramita is patience, which also has three types. The first type of patience is tolerance, to not be offended by harm. If someone beats, hurts, robs, or defeats you, or abuses you with nasty words, do not retaliate with anger or hatred, but instead cultivate loving kindness. The second is the patience of gladly undergoing hardship when seeking teachings or practicing. When actually practicing the teachings in circumstances where you may be too hot, cold, hungry, thirsty or tired, do not lose courage, but instead generate fortitude.

The third patience is open-minded trust. Do not be afraid or timid when hearing about the resolve of past conquerors and bodhisattvas, or their inconceivable great qualities, or about the natural state of emptiness, or the profound methods. Repeatedly generate delight and take joy in all of these. When some of the arhats of the past heard about emptiness—that everything is nonexistent, illusory—out of their resistance, they fainted. They simply did not want to hear about it. Likewise, have an open mind when hearing about the Buddha's past lives, his five hundred inferior rebirths, his five hundred superior rebirths, and what he did in all those past lives before becoming a fully enlightened buddha. Instead of immediately closing one's mind and saying, "No way, that could not have any meaning," have some trust, and think, "Hey, maybe it was something very good." In addition, for other kinds of teachings, like those on profound emptiness, do not shut them out, but generate unprejudiced trust. To be unafraid of the profound truth is the third type of patience.

Next is perseverance or diligence, which also has three types. First is the armorlike diligence, which means, when practicing, not to belittle the importance of a small virtuous action by thinking, "This is unnecessary. It does not matter." Similarly, when a practice is very great, do not lose courage or think, "I cannot do that. It is beyond me." Genuinely take delight in practicing any type of goodness, no matter what it is. The second type is the diligence of constant application.

When practicing anything that is true and good, do not give in to laziness and distraction, but instead continue with some constancy. The third type is the diligence of not turning back, which is not to lose faith or courage even if there are no immediate signs in your practice. Instead, see the value and carry on until reaching the final result.

The training is in the pledge that "I will train in these four paramitas to the best of my ability."

Shamatha with Support

I will now explain in more detail the second part involving concentration, which is dhyana, the fifth paramita. There are two aspects: the causes for bringing forth concentration, and the actual concentration itself.

Since dhyana and shamatha are of identical nature, here is how to bring forth the support that is the cause for producing concentration. Keep your body away from distractions by finding a quiet place. Moreover, keep your mind away from conceptual thinking. Distractions are children, spouse, friends, and followers—basically all sentient beings. Likewise, further distractions are food, wealth, honor, gain, praise, fame, and a good reputation. To cling to any of these is a diversion. This being so, in a sutra the Buddha has taught the twenty shortcomings of attachment to diversions.[19] The negative side of distractions is that they prevent the mind from simply remaining at ease. Distractions are that which diverts your attention whenever you try to sit down calmly. They capture your attention and draw you away from your practice. That is the definition of a distraction.

A remote place is somewhere free of these diversions. Having given up distractions, remain alone in a remote place, in a retreat. The Tibetan word for retreat is actually *gompa*, and these days the monasteries have the name gompa. Actually, gompa means a place far away from the city or the village, or at least removed a certain distance from settlements. The Buddha has taught the benefit of retreat as being that it will quickly allow samadhi to take birth in your stream of being. When remaining in a remote place, your body and voice can be employed in virtuous actions and practice. However, being in solitude will not bring much benefit if you physically and verbally make yourself busy or pursue negative or pointless activities while staying in a quiet place. You are just giving another name to being in a distracted state. Abandon all those things. We can also make our minds emotionally disturbed by various kinds of thinking, becoming caught up in subtle or coarse thoughts. Give this up. Without distracting yourself in any way, one-pointedly train in shamatha and concentration. This is how samadhi will take birth in your being. That was the preparation.

Now comes the actual training in dhyana or concentration. The way to begin is by the first type of dhyana, the dhyana of peacefully abiding in actuality. Apply that presently in this life, not in some future life. Do so by developing pliancy of body and mind. In this context, there are certain physical and mental key points to implement. The first has to do with posture.

There are two ways to place the body: one with effort, the other effortless. These two types of body postures are used in both Mahamudra and Dzogchen—they are basically the same. The effortless posture means to leave the legs loosely crossed in the *sattva* posture and rest the hands freely on the knees. This is called the 'position of mental ease.' You are neither too tight nor too relaxed.

The deliberate or effortful posture is described as the 'sevenfold posture of Vairochana.' There are seven points to it. First, cross the legs like a vajra [this is commonly known as full lotus]. Straighten the spine like a pillar, so that it is perfectly erect, with one vertebra directly on top of the next. Extend the shoulders like the wings of a vulture, and bend the neck slightly like a hook. Keep the tongue touching the upper palate, the lips and teeth slightly parted, and hold the gaze at a forty-five degree angle in the direction of the tip of the nose.

There is a reason why we place the body in a particular position. Keeping the meditation posture affects the energy currents, of which there are five major and 21,600 minor currents. The five major currents are known as the upward-moving, the downward-clearing, the equalizing, the life-force sustaining, and the pervading currents. When the key points of the vajra body are activated, then these five primary currents automatically become currents of the wisdom winds, the winds of original wakefulness. This has to do with how, at some point, the materiality of the physical being disperses into rainbow light. There are many other reasons for each aspect of the sevenfold posture of Vairochana—primarily the specific way it affects the function of and the direct interaction it has with the energy currents. Of course, we could study all this, but the main benefit has to do with attaining the rainbow body.

There is an oral tradition that says when the body is straightened, the channels are straight, and when the channels are straight the energy currents flow freely. When the currents flow freely, the state of mind is suspended in naturalness. Body posture can have a direct effect on your state of mind. When all the energy currents flow freely in a certain position, it is called 'the solitude of body.' When we suspend all verbal articulation and utterance, remaining silent with a particular type of free-flowing breathing, it is called 'the solitude of speech.' The energy currents are called the karma winds, and are interconnected with our mind and thought activity—all our concepts of good and evil, pleasant and unpleasant, hope and fear, and so on. When this particular body posture affects the flow of currents, the mental state eases into naturalness, which is called 'the solitude of mind.' Taken together, these are considered 'the threefold solitude of body, speech and mind.'

These points all have to do with the actual physical posture of settling your body and positioning it. Neither be too tight nor too relaxed. There is a medium balance between the two.

The way to begin meditation practice in this context is by using a support for the attention. Eventually, you go on to having no support, resting in unsupported concentration.

For the first of these, use Arya Tara as a support. This could be in the form of a painting or statue, but it should be of the correct proportions and of fine quality. Place the image in front of you so that you can direct your attention to the figure of Tara. If you do not have a physical statue or painting, it is fine to simply visualize what Tara looks like. As the root text states:

> In particular, straighten your body, expel your stale
>   breath.
> Your focus, in the sky before you, is the form of Jetsün
>   Tara,
> Inseparable from your guru.

The nature of your guru is in the form of Tara. She is green like the purest emerald, brilliant, clear, radiant, and surrounded by five-colored light shining in all directions. She is peacefully smiling, with her right hand resting upon her right knee in the gesture of supreme giving, the right arm extended. In front of her heart center, her left hand holds, between the thumb and the ring finger, the stem of a blue lotus in full bloom at the level of her left ear. Her hair is loosely styled. At the top of her head, some braids are tied together with a huge shining jewel, the rest of the hair flowing freely down her back. She wears the various types of jewelry. First is her crown, adorned with different jewels. She wears earrings, necklaces, bracelets, anklets and a jeweled belt. The silken ornaments include the upper covering and the lower garment. Her right leg is slightly extended, while the left is slightly bent. She sits upon a white lotus and moon disc. This is how to visualize her.

This specific practice is taught by all the buddhas to help focus your attention and achieve stillness of mind. There are other methods you could use, but one particular way is to use a form of an awakened being, such as Tara, as a support for nondistraction. It is not the same as the visualization practice, where you have the three principles of stable pride, vivid presence and pure recollection of the symbolism. The image here is a support to avoid getting distracted by other things. Simply let your attention rest on the image, without speculating about whether it is correct or incorrect, good or not good.

Jamgön Kongtrül explains that you simply use this as a support for capturing the attention. Do not worry whether it is vivid or dull, precise or vague, whether the mind rests or does not rest, and so forth. You should completely abandon any such hope, fear, worry or concern. Simply keep mindfulness on guard against getting distracted and wandering off.

When you are neither dull nor agitated, but poised, then rest your eyes at the level of Tara's heart center and simply remain settled in equanimity. If dullness, drowsiness, or murkiness is more predominant, raise your attention to between Tara's eyebrows, and simply focus there. If you feel agitated and disturbed, imagine a small blue sphere at the level of her navel and lower your eyes slightly. In all cases, focus your mind, eyes, and breath together one-pointedly, just as you do when you thread a needle. With such focused attention there is a one-pointedness that is undistracted. Train in this for a short period, but repeat it many times. As soon as you notice that you have wandered off, bring your attention back and again let it rest. By training in this repeatedly, the attention eventually is captured. When it has been caught, you simply remain there, undistracted, very relaxed and naturally, for as long as you can sustain it. At the end of the session, imagine that the form of the deity before you melts into light and is absorbed into you, so that the guru, Arya Tara's mind and your own mind are indivisibly of one taste, and then remain in the equanimity.

When training in this way, the main point is short periods repeated many times. Every time you feel drowsy or tired, raise your eyes and imagine that there is a little white sphere between Tara's eyes. When you feel disturbed or restless, lower your gaze and imagine that there is a small blue sphere at Tara's navel. When neither disturbed nor drowsy, simply rest your gaze at the level of her heart. By practicing in this way, you will develop quietness of mind. At the end of the session, just as before, settle into the state of equanimity totally free of any mental constructs of the three spheres, as explained earlier.

This concludes the section on shamatha with support.

Shamatha without Support

In the previous section, I explained how to use the form of Arya Tara as the support for being undistracted in the development of dhyana, concentration. The next training is in developing concentration without using any support.

Here, Jamgön Kongtrül continues to explain that in order to develop concentration without using a support, assume the posture as in the previous practice. Exhale the stale breath. Then instead of keeping something in mind, simply interrupt any thinking about whatever occurs in the three times: past, present, and future. In other words, you do not ruminate over what has taken place previously, nor do you plan or anticipate anything that might happen in the future. Neither should you try to improve, modify or adjust your awareness in the present moment. Do not try to eliminate anything or encourage anything. Simply keep a lucid and undistracted awareness. The main point is to remain undistracted without doing anything else.

Previously, I mentioned that when you feel drowsy you should raise your gaze up to the place between Tara's eyes. If you feel agitated, you may lower the gaze to the navel. When you feel balanced, leave the gaze at Tara's heart. In this case, you may continue to raise or lower your gaze, but no other focus needs to be kept in mind. The main point is to simply allow your awareness to be very gentle and serene. Each time you do so, the thought flow, the involvement in thoughts, is interrupted. When you get distracted, merely come back to resting like that again.

Train like this over and over, but in such a way that you do not grow tired of it.

By training in this way, you will sometimes see things with your eyes or hear sounds with your ears that generate thoughts. Sensory experiences occur, based on the five senses, which stimulate thoughts. When that happens, do not follow up on the thought, but leave your attention right there. Take whatever you see or hear as a support and let your attention remain on it, instead of flying off to the next thing. By doing this, any sound, sight, or other potential distraction can be used as a support for the quietude and calmness of the mind.

When you get too agitated, distracted or restless, or you feel bored or tired of this, do not try to calm down the mind or stop it from being agitated. If suddenly the mind gets too restless and wants to think of something, let the attention go to that. But whatever it goes to, leave the attention on that, rather than jumping to a second or third subject. You are somewhat allowing thoughts to occur, but you do not jump onto the next. Merely sustain the awareness of what you think of. In doing so, you alternate between remaining with whatever occurs, and thinking of something and then remaining with that.

Usually in this kind of practice you go back and forth between being focused and being relaxed. There is some fluctuation between those two. As you grow more accustomed, you do not fluctuate too much between being too concentrated or too tight and too loose. You cultivate a more balanced way of sustaining awareness. Once you get to that, there are certain stages that you go through, three of which are mentioned here. The first one is said to be like a waterfall in the mountains, the second like a peacefully flowing river, and the third like an ocean free of waves. In the beginning, it feels like there is a continuous stream of thoughts. It is somewhat violent—one thing, then the next and the next and the next and the next, continually. You think, "Do I actually get so occupied with thinking? I never used to have thoughts like this." In the meditation state, you discover how much your mind churns out thoughts. It is usually like this—it did not just happen because you started to meditate. Now, you finally become aware of the flow of thought that has been taking place all the time. This is the first level of experience in shamatha. As you simply let go and train with that, it diminishes. The rush eases off, to become more like the gentle flow of a river. That is the second level. Eventually the thoughts become less and less and less, until the mind is like a placid ocean undisturbed by waves.

The practice up to this point is called planting the roots or laying the foundation for all subsequent meditation. Samadhi, vipashyana, and so forth are henceforth possible, as you have prepared yourself in this way. All the different practices that follow have a platform or a root from which they can grow. The instructions up to this point belong to the first type of dhyana.

The second type of dhyana is 'the dhyana that produces the virtuous qualities.' This means any kind of pursuit that you have in meditation practice. All of these states of samadhi that produce specific qualities, called 'emancipations', 'subjugations', 'perception spheres', 'totalities', and so forth, now become possible due to your having laid this foundation. The third type of dhyana is called 'the dhyana that accomplishes the welfare of sentient beings.' It has to do with the samadhis, clairvoyance, and the superknowledges, by means of which you can actually help others. Developing both the second and third types of dhyana require having perfected the first type.

PRAJÑA

Now we have come to the sixth paramita—insight, *sherab* in Tibetan or prajña in Sanskrit. Please understand that this prajña is, in essence, exactly the same as the awakened state of all buddhas. It is the intelligence that fully discerns all phenomena; in that sense, it is not different from the awakened state. It manifests due to the accumulation of merit. As Shantideva says, "All the Buddha's teachings are simply for the purpose of prajña." Jamgön Kongtrül places his explanation under two headings: intent and application.

The intent has three parts. Initially it is the knowledge of the ultimate, which is realization of emptiness, the natural state. Subsequently, there is knowledge of the relative, which is to clearly understand how all knowable things are in their identities, and the connection between causes and effects and dependent origination. Thirdly, there is the intelligence of how to benefit beings, which is carrying out the four means of magnetizing, and so forth.

The application can also be divided into three sections. First, there is the training in the absence of personal identity; next, the training in the absence of identity of phenomena or things and finally, the training in the emptiness suffused with compassion, or the emptiness with the heart of compassion. In this way, all the great treatises and scriptures teach exactly the same thing. This is called 'establishing certainty in the view.' This is the kind of knowledge that is necessary to understand.

There is much more to study about these topics, but now we are going to train in a particular type of prajña—how to produce the wakefulness of vipashyana.

Vipashyana

In this context, the insight of vipashyana is produced by realizing the natural state. This type of vipashyana is an insight that comes after having understood how things actually are. I will explain how to realize the nature of things according to the approach taken by Atisha. The substance of the training is none other than the wisdom of vipashyana brought fully forth. After realizing it, you can then truly train in vipashyana, which has two aspects: inquiring what the nature of things actually is, and then settling in the natural state.

Inquiry has three aspects. First, inquire into externally perceived objects. Next, inquire into the inner perceiving mind. Lastly, seek and investigate the very identity or nature of this mind.

Regarding investigation into the perceived objects that are external, the Buddha says in *The Lankavatara Sutra,* "The mind that is churned by habitual tendencies is seen as if it were various objects. In actuality, these are not objects, but the mind itself. So, to see objects as being external is mistaken." In the *Avatamsaka Sutra*, the Buddha says something like, "Hey, children of the conquerors, the three realms are only mind." As the root text states:

Within this state, all that appears
As outer and inner, the world and beings,
Is merely personal perception, like dreaming.

Endless quotations substantiate this principle, both in the words of the Buddha and in the treatises of Buddhist masters. That which is regarded as the outer world, formed of the four elements, as well as the beings living in it who appear through the four types of rebirth, are all experienced by deluded mind as if they were external. In actuality, apart from these confused perceptions, there is not even as much as an atom that truly exists outside. It is like this example: while dreaming, you may see mountains, walls, houses, men and women, horses, and cattle, and so forth, in all different shapes and forms. There can be pleasure and pain, joy and sorrow, fear and anxiety—but no matter what you dream of, it is nothing but a dream. Such phenomena are merely perceptions that take place within deluded mind, apart from which they have no real existence. Though the state of dreaming is intrinsically unreal, we still dream. Due to not knowing that it is a dream, all the various emotions—joy and sorrow, fear and anxiety—are experienced as real.

Our present perceptions are similarly unreal and insubstantial. They unfold and function within the experience of deluded mind. The whole falsehood of relative delusion collapses once you understand and recognize that they are false and mistaken, and you understand that all appearances are simply your own mind. This is the understanding to arrive at. Be persistent in inquiring and examining in this way.

That was about external objects. Now, let's address the inner perceiving mind. If the perceived objects are all mind, shouldn't the mind itself actually exist? Shouldn't the perceiving mind within be real? Actually, mind has no reality or concreteness whatsoever, because the stream of mind is not composed of either singular or multiple moments. This stream of mind is not perceptible by anyone. It cannot be seen. It has no location. Therefore, you cannot prove that there is such a thing as 'mind.' In *The Sutra Requested by Kashyapa*, the Buddha says, "Kashyapa, mind is not inside or outside. Nor can it be found anywhere between the two. Kashyapa, mind is not something you can scrutinize, nor can it be shown. It is not supported by anything. It is not visible. It is not perceptible. It does not remain anywhere. Kashyapa, this mind has never been seen, is not being seen and will never be seen, even by all the buddhas."

What we label 'mind' is, in fact, just an occurrence of thought that suddenly appears and in the next moment completely vanishes. Besides that, there is no thing there whatsoever. It is comparable to how a cloud forms in the sky and vanishes without a trace, simply disappearing within the empty expanse. Similarly, in the empty, natural state, a thought occurs and naturally vanishes. This seemingly continual arising and ceasing fools all sentient beings, for, in actuality, within emptiness there is no thing whatsoever. The sudden arising of a moment of knowing is thought of as being 'me' and clung to as being 'I.' That ego is believed to be the personal identity. This so-called 'self' does not possess even the slightest substance indicating a true existence. Please inquire and look carefully into your own experience, until you fully realize that this is so. Decisively and from deep within your heart, you should be very certain that there is no real personal identity.

The first inquiry covered the absence of identity of phenomena, and the second was the inquiry into the absence of personal identity. Now, the third inquiry involves seeking and investigating the nature of this mind.

Since there is no basis whatsoever for assigning the labels 'personal identity' and 'the identity of phenomena,' in that there is not anything that can be verified and proven, you may think, "Well then, there is nothing at all. It is only a void nature of mind, nothingness." However, this is not the case. That the perceiver and perceived have no concrete existence does not mean that there is a complete nothingness. To maintain so would involve assigning a new label, such as 'inconcrete' because of not being concrete. All phenomena are from the very beginning unverifiable, by their very nature. Whether something is concrete or not is merely a matter of conceptual labeling. Reality transcends both. As the Buddha said in *The Lankavatara Sutra*, "Just as external objects that are neither concrete nor inconcrete, so is the mind. It cannot be held as having substantial existence. Therefore, 'nonarising nature' means to have given up every opinion."

In addition, in the *Prajñaparamita*, the Buddha says, "Mind does not exist as mind, but as a nature that is luminous wakefulness." This luminosity refers to the naked quality that is able to know. Even though it is not a 'thing', there is still an unimpeded ability to know. That is called luminosity—empty, yet able to know. Saraha says, "To hold the opinion that mind is concrete is to be like an ox. But to hold the opinion that it is inconcrete is to be even more foolish." Accordingly, when you inquire into the very identity of your own mind, you cannot find any 'thing', because it does not have any physical form, shape, or color; it is not a material entity with defining marks. Nothing supports that. Likewise, you cannot maintain the opinion that there is nothing at all, because there is a knowing that forms the basis for any experience belonging to samsara or nirvana. In other words, there is a lucid quality that is simply conscious or aware, unceasingly.

This being so, we may then form the opinion that there are many kinds of minds. Yet this does not hold up either, because all of them are of the same taste or nature, being emptiness. As all moments of experiences are equally empty, there are not many kinds. Moreover, you cannot say that there is only one mind, because there are so many kinds of experiences possible, such as those of the five senses and the mental field. In other words, how the reality of experience actually *is* defies any conceptual constructs that we may form about it. This inquiry is to recognize how the nature of mind truly is.

Settling into the Natural State

We have now investigated external objects and personal identity, what is considered this 'me' that perceives. By doing this, we have become certain that these are not to be found anywhere. In short, we are unable to prove a concrete reality of anything whatsoever. This is what such inquiry is for—discovering the natural state, what is real. Now we need to settle in that, which is the second section. It is how to just be that way. Kongtrül explains that the settling evenly in the continuity of the natural state is *after* having investigated by means of discriminating intelligence in the previous way, and *after* having achieved some certainty in how reality is; it is to settle in equanimity within that certainty. As Shantideva says, "Once you do not hold in mind any concept of anything as being concrete or inconcrete, at that point, you do not need to hold anything else in mind, but simply remain utterly peaceful and without concepts." Having discovered that everything is like a rainbow or magical illusion, that there is no concrete reality to the perceiver or the perceived, you do not need to form any extraneous opinion. Simply remain like that, utterly peaceful.

The way to practice this is to keep the sevenfold posture, the same posture as before, and exhale the stale breath. Through training in shamatha, you have already acquired a sense of ease, of remaining free of concepts and yet quite lucid. Beyond these attributes, you do not have to establish or exclude, adopt or avoid anything whatsoever. Simply divest or divorce yourself of any opinion. You do not need to produce a thought about anything. You do not have to speculate about anything. Simply allow your attention to be as it is, free of all constructs. In other words, remain naturally, like a totally clear, wide-open sky, and allow that to continue. Simply remain in that.

Vipashyana here is not some particular insight that you try to keep. In shamatha, the mind is somewhat settled and calm. Now, through inquiry, there is a seeing of how this mind actually is—that there is neither perceiver nor perceived really existing anywhere. To simply see what is real is called insight and given the label 'vipashyana.' It does not mean fabricating or holding any understanding in mind whatsoever. It is nonfabrication, merely allowing the natural state to continue. Vipashyana is nothing other than simply being natural and continuing in that way.

In the text called *The Precious Treasury of Nonarising,* Longchen Rabjam states, "When you do not conceptualize anything whatsoever and you do not speculate in any way, to simply be uncontrived is the precious treasury of nonarising." In other words, complete nonfabrication.

Among all the various instructions, the guidance in vipashyana is exactly this, the nonfabrication. During the state of composure, there is actually no thing being meditated upon or cultivated yet, at the same time, you are not to be distracted from that for even one instant. You simply settle in your natural state that is lucid and aware, and maintain its continuity. This was about the state of composure.

In postmeditation, you regard whatever you perceive, all appearances and perceptions, as being a magical illusion, or like a dream. You keep that assurance, that confidence. At the same time, you regard with compassion all other sentient beings that are continuously involved in experiencing samsaric suffering due to mistakenly believing in themselves and appearances as being real. They have not understood the natural state or the reality of emptiness. All these beings are your own parents. There is a deepfelt compassion towards all of them that is indivisible from this emptiness, free of perceiver and perceived. Endeavor in this until you attain confidence in the nature of reality, your innate state. This transcendent knowledge, *prajñaparamita*, is the ultimate Arya Tara. In this way you come face to face with the ultimate Tara; you meet the real Tara.

To reiterate, during the meditation session you simply remain without speculating, without forming any concepts whatsoever. Remain completely natural and uncontrived. Then, during postmeditation—meaning during daily activity—try never to lose the attitude that all of this is like a dream or a magical illusion. In this way, compassion for others arises from within this state of emptiness free of perceiver and perceived. This compassion is completely spontaneous and unfabricated. By growing increasingly accustomed to this training during composure and postmeditation, you will eventually recognize the ultimate Tara, *prajñaparamita*, transcendent knowledge.

In some teachings, it is said that through intelligent inquiry, you discover that there is no real basis to the perceiver or the perceived—in other words, you discover emptiness. Settling into that assurance, you still need to retain a very subtle understanding of emptiness. For if you let that slip, then there is no difference between just settling there and shamatha without support.

However, in my opinion, once you have gone through the intellectual inquiry, have discovered the lack of perceiver and perceived, and have gained the assurance that there is no thing there to hold in mind, you do not need on top of that to hold in mind the idea that they are devoid of true existence. That is definitely not required. There is no danger of losing anything, because once you have realized this that is it. This does not mean you should stray into forgetting through thinking about something else, either. As long as you are not distracted, you do not have to keep the conceptual idea of emptiness during the composure, the meditation state. Nonetheless, during the postmeditation state, when you interact with others, you should continuously bring to mind the notion that all of this is like a dream. All of this is like a magical illusion.

This concludes the stages of instruction and the trainings that correspond to the medium type of person.

The Excellence of the End—
Vajrayana

We come now to the excellence of the end, the explanation of the path for the superior type of person. This involves applying the unexcelled secret teachings of the Vajra vehicle, Vajrayana practice itself. Previously, I explained how to meet Tara through the Mahayana path. Now, by applying the skillful methods of Vajrayana, you can fully realize Tara and become Tara in actuality.

These teachings are presented under three headings or sections. First is how to practice the 'approach' aspect, through gathering the accumulations in conformity with the outer way according to the Kriya and Charya tantras. Next, the manner of 'accomplishment' in conformity with Yoga Tantra is elucidated, which is the receiving of blessings. Thirdly, the innermost way of practice is shown, which is in accordance with Anuttara Yoga and is the path of the complete four empowerments.[20]

Approach

As to how to practice the approach according to the Kriya and Charya tantras, I will present the general explanation, then the specific guidance on how to practice.

First, for the general explanation, please understand that these teachings are presented in a gradual manner. Each of the nine vehicles is explained in very organized fashion, one after the other. The purpose of previous teachings is to guide your stream of being and prepare you for the next level of teaching. We train in purifying our minds as a preparation. For example, the main part of the previous Mahayana practice was to establish the foundation or the root for the entire path—the view and the training in emptiness.

Now comes something superior to the view and meditation presented above. This is a gradual way of training in Vajrayana, which is vastly advanced in relation to the previous and has an immense intent. This great purpose is stated in a Vajrayana text called *The Compendium*: "Through this the indivisible three kayas, the identity of the Bhagavan [meaning Buddhahood itself], adorned with the ocean of wisdoms, will be achieved within this same lifetime." Within that perspective, the practices that correspond to the Kriya and Charya tantras are called the outer sadhana while Yoga Tantra is the inner sadhana of Tara. They are said to be like the limbs—the arms and the legs—whereas the main body is the Anuttara Yoga tantra because it has both the development and completion stages.

In *The Subsequent Compendium Tantra,* there is a statement supporting this: "The Dharma taught by every buddha is included in twofold stages. One is the development stage and the other is the completion stage." We begin with the development stage to purify our clinging to the world and beings as ordinary. Next, we practice the completion stage in order to attain the supreme unity of bliss and emptiness by binding the winds and mind within the indestructible sphere. This practice unfolds from the nonarising emptiness that was previously explained as the view. It is within the continuity of this view that the unimpeded play of experience is allowed to take form as the samadhi of the threefold mandala. This is how it is taught.

The Ritual of the Four Mandalas

At this point, it is advantageous to learn the ritual of the four mandalas of *Zabtik Drölma*, *The Profound Essence of Tara*. This text comes in right here. It is called the Tara practice of the original four mandalas, and I will concisely explain how to practice this.

Prepare one mandala and put it on the shrine. The other three mandalas come in the text itself, by offering the mandala three times. The way to begin this practice is to clean your environment. Position an image of Arya Tara, either a statue or a painting, on the shrine. In front of that put the general offerings. They should all be made as tidy and clean as possible. Wash your five extremities—your feet, your hands and face. Before doing this practice, you must avoid improper food including meat, alcohol, onions and garlic. You only partake of the three whites [milk, curd and ghee]. Abide by untainted behavior and motivate yourself with renunciation and the will to be free of samsara. Develop a compassionate attitude towards all sentient beings.

Begin the practice by repeating the lines for taking refuge. Next, generate the bodhichitta resolve, then offer the seven branches for gathering the accumulations. Having done that as a prelude, in a single instant imagine yourself in the form of Arya Tara. In your heart center, upon a moon disc, is the syllable TAM, of green color, radiating rays of light. Because of these rays of light, from Tara's pure realm, known as Arrayed in Turquoise Petals, Arya Tara appears with twenty manifestations in a circle around her. Additionally, an infinite number of the Three Jewels emerge. They are invited to remain in the sky before you, and are seated upon their individual seats of lotus and moon discs. Imagine that you present the two water offerings [for drinking and rinsing], the general offerings of sense-pleasures, and either the extensive or concise mandala offerings, whichever is appropriate. After that repeat the praise, in the form of the twenty-one praises twice.

Next, focus on Tara's right hand, which is in the gesture of bestowing protection. Pray that you and all others to be protected come under her hand and are relieved from every type of fear. Once again, offer a mandala and repeat the twenty-one praises three times. From the bodily forms of the central figure and all of Tara's retinue of the twenty Taras, a stream of nectar appears that enters the crown of your head as well as the heads of all beings to be protected. Imagine that your body fills with nectar and that your stream of being is completely filled with the blessings of enlightened body, speech and mind. While visualizing this, offer another mandala and the twenty-one praises seven times. Finally, Tara, together with her retinue, melts into light that dissolves into you, so that the deity and you are indivisible. Be confident that you are fully blessed.

Next, chant the ten-syllable Tara mantra as many times as you can. [OM TARE TUTTARE TURE SOHA]. When done, settle evenly into the original, natural state in which the deity and your own mind are indivisible. After a while, dedicate the merit and recite the verses of auspiciousness. That is the general sequence of practice. If you practice like this for as few as three days or seven days, repeatedly and with perseverance, it will pacify outer and inner obstacles and fulfill whatever virtuous wishes you have.

This is called the approach style, which is the outer sadhana of gathering the accumulations. That is the general sequence of the Tara practice.

There is a tendency to always want the easy way. Samten Gyatso, the guru of Tulku Urgyen Rinpoche, would place five mandalas on his shrine. Even though the name of the practice is the Four Mandalas, he would have five. He would have a mandala and a tripod covered with a piece of brocade, on top of which he would put the Tara statue. In the four directions around it, he would place four mandala plates. Every time the mandala offering was made, somebody would replenish the offering on the mandala plates. These days it doesn't seem like people are doing that. They have only one mandala and when the time comes, they replenish the offerings on top of that one. This is how it often goes. Moreover, people are supposed to sound the cymbals, but they think it is much easier to ring their bells, and so they omit them. Yet, if that is how we let the tradition go, everything gets watered down. Samten Gyatso never allowed that tendency at all. He wanted to be precise. Nobody was allowed to skip anything at all. He would be extremely meticulous.

This *Zabtik Drölma* practice is very widespread. People do it all the way from Amdo throughout Tibet. All the Kagyü centers in the West practice this, and in other countries as well. It is an extremely pervasive text. However, they do not know who composed it, because often there is no colophon at the end. Some think it was Kongtrül, others think it is a tantra. They are not sure which it is.

ACCOMPLISHMENT

Now comes practicing the inner manner of sadhana, the 'accomplishment' style, which is in accordance with Yoga Tantra. Begin by laying out the shrine articles appropriately, as the text describes. Wash your body and keep it clean. Your motivation should be pure, as always. Recite the refuge prayer, take the bodhisattva vow, and gather the accumulations, in the same way as before. When you come to the main sadhana itself, there is something extra to be inserted at this point. There are three parts I will explain: the preparation, the eminent sadhana arrangement, and finally the sequence of activities.

In the more detailed sadhanas there are many particulars, but here only the protection circle is added, so visualize the protection circle. By means of the shunyata mantra,[21] dissolve all outer and inner phenomena into emptiness. From within the continuity of emptiness, the radiance of your own mind, everything unfolds. Initially, the green syllable TAM appears. It appears suddenly, vividly, and brilliantly, like a shooting star in the center of space. Imagine that this dazzling green syllable TAM is the only thing in the immensity of space. Swiftly it emits sound—not as a form, but simply as sound. This sound is HUNG, which resonates like roaring thunder. The sound of HUNG invokes the nature of all buddhas. It captures their attention.

The HUNG sound also eliminates any kind of interference from negative forces that could possibly arise. All these are cut short immediately. The immense brilliance of the rays of light shining from the HUNG sound takes the form of a rain that showers down from all directions. The raindrops then turn into the shapes of vajras. These slowly arrange themselves in particular patterns. First is called the vajra ground, second the vajra fence, third the vajra dome. They are everywhere—below, all around, and above. Jamgön Kongtrül explains that they create a sphere so completely impenetrable that not even the cosmic storm at the end of a kalpa can blow through. In other words, it is completely safe and secure in all directions.

For the vajra ground, the first drop that turns into a vajra becomes an immense vajra cross, like two crossed vajras. It is so large that the four points extend to the ends of the universe. Imagine that in between the openings there are further vajra crosses in sizes that correspond to what can fit. Smaller, smaller, and even smaller ones are placed, until there is a huge platform of vajra crosses that meld together so that the smallest one is even tinier than a mustard seed. The surface underneath is like the spokes of the vajra, while on top, they are completely smooth like polished silver and totally impenetrable. It feels thoroughly level, but you can still see the shapes inside. That is the first aspect, the vajra ground.

The vajra fence is like when a herdsman in the mountains builds a night shelter for his animals, constructing an enclosure of vertically aligned bamboo all around them. In this way, you imagine that the raindrops become vajras that are vertical, standing side by side far out in the distance at the ends of the vajra cross. They are enormous. They stand up there, five prongs, nine prongs, and so forth, like a colossal wall. In between there are smaller vajras, down to the tiniest size, so that on the outside the structure has the shape of vajras and on the inside it is totally smooth. This is the vajra fence.

Above that is the vajra dome, which can be visualized in various ways. On top of the vajra fence is a ring of vajras, where half of it sticks outside, half inside. They are also gigantic and form a single circle. On top of them is another ring, then another one, until finally one stands in the middle. Again, it is very smooth on the inside and has the shape of vajras on the outside. Inside this is a lattice for a canopy; another lattice hangs on the outside for the garlands and some loops and pendants, which are also formed of vajras. The main point is that the vajra dome is of immense dimensions, impenetrable.

Other sadhanas put various things on the outside and inside, but this is the simple form of the vajra ground, fence and dome. You imagine that it goes down from the biggest dimension into the finest detail. There is not even a single opening; it is completely smooth on the inside. That was the preparation, the protection circle.

Now comes the second part, which is the main sequence of the sadhana. From within the protection circle you imagine according to the general manner. On top of the mandalas for wind, fire, water and earth, Mount Sumeru rises in the center. The mandala for wind is crescent-shaped and immense. Above is the mandala for fire, which is triangular. The mandala for water is circular, and the mandala for earth is square. On top of that is Mount Sumeru. Each of the four sides is in a different color.

On top of Mount Sumeru is the syllable DHRUNG, which all of a sudden turns into a celestial palace. This palace is likewise enormous but still fits inside the vajra enclosure. It has four sides, with four portals in the four directions. The palace is the universal type of mandala temple with all the generally known details and attributes. In the center is a multicolored lotus flower with eight gigantic petals and anthers with pistils in the middle. They support a huge, flat moon disc. Bring each of these features to mind one by one. This is called the 'mandala of the support.'

The mandala temple or celestial palace is situated on Mount Sumeru and is made of jeweled light. It is exquisite, utterly perfect, with amazing decorations and characteristics. If you do not know the specific details, you use what is called the general mandala temple of Vajrasattva according to the Nyingma tradition. It is a square temple with each side in a different color. There is a gate and set of doors in each of the four directions. In front of each doorway is a portal, which could be in triple, double, or singular form, with a multitude of details. It is called the eightfold portal.

Please remember that every single aspect of the mandala temple has a specific purpose, meaning, and symbolism. The dimensions of the temple are based on the shape of the deity, as the temple is a manifestation of the deity. That is where the proportions of the temple come from. Whether it is several stories or not depends on the specific deity. Since Tara is a single figure, this temple has one storey above, with pillars and beams, and the roof with the jewel top ornament at the center.

Inside the center of the palace is a massive lotus flower with eight petals. It is called a 'multi-lotus'. It could be visualized in various ways according to the particular sadhanas, for example with each petal being a different color. Here, every petal shines with multicolored light. There are actually two sets of petals, an outer one and a somewhat flat one within that, whose shape sticks up a little bit. The anthers and pistils of the lotus support the moon disc, which is as wide as the pistils extend. The moon disc is usually painted completely flat, according to the convenience of the painter, whereas in actuality the ends bend up a little bit. Sometimes the lotus, sun and moon discs fit together in a certain way. All of this has a profound symbolism.

Next comes the 'mandala of the supported,' which is the deity. The syllable TAM that you visualized in the beginning descends over the center of the throne on the lotus and moon disc, landing right in the center of the moon disc. It immediately turns into another green lotus, an *utpala* lotus flower with the syllable TAM in the center. It is brilliant, with shining rays of light emanating in all directions. These rays of light purify all the realms of sentient beings and carry out all the buddha activities. The immense light rays return back into the TAM syllable, which instantly changes into the bodily form of Tara. It transforms so that you become Tara. The color of the body, what is held in the hands, and the ornaments are all the same as I previously explained. Her radiant and graceful countenance is luminous, visible yet insubstantial. She is a Sambhogakaya buddha with the thirteen Sambhogakaya garments and ornaments. She has the complete thirty-two major and eighty minor marks of excellence according to the general description. All of these are perfect and complete. She is radiant, dignified and brilliant. Most importantly, she is able to be seen yet intangible, like a rainbow in the sky. Visualize the form of Tara as evident but not material.

Inside the heart center, you visualize the green syllable TAM. The syllable is situated sideways[22] and sends out eight similar TAM syllables, as the text says, four into the cardinal directions and four into the intermediate directions. They each land on their own petal of an eight-petalled lotus flower.

As they stand there, they send out rays of light that alleviate the eight outer and eight inner fears. The eight outer fears have to do with outer situations, while the inner fears are the eight negative emotions and negative viewpoints, such as the idea of a "me," or the idea of "forever," or "nothing at all." There are eight negative emotional states that are the root of every anxiety. All of these are pacified by means of the rays of light from these eight TAM syllables. Not only are the sixteen fears pacified, but also the light then establishes every sentient being in the same noble state as Tara herself.

As the light returns back, each of the TAM syllables becomes a full-fledged form of Tara, each a separate color, and each holding different things in her hands. The first one is visualized in the eastern direction, in front, then one after the other in a clockwise direction are the other Taras. The first of these eight is called the 'Tara who protects against the eight fears.' Outside these, you imagine that this whole lotus is resting on a big platform or podium, which has four corners. On the outer edge of these, there are another four corners, so there are actually eight areas where eight goddesses are situated. The first four are Lila, Mala, Girti and Nirti. They are the four inner goddesses. Outside these are the Sanskrit names for incense, flower, lamp and perfume so that altogether there are eight goddesses. At each of the four doorways of the mandala, in each of the four directions, are four goddesses who have the names for hook, chain, shackle and bell.

All of this constitutes the mandala of twenty-one forms of Tara. Each manifestation has her specific color, expression, ornaments and attributes, and all are complete and perfect. They are to be visualized as the profound brilliance of nondual, original wakefulness. That means that the bodily form of the deity, the palace—everything—is actually bliss indivisible from emptiness. It also means that whatever is seen is indivisible from emptiness—insubstantial, yet visible. All the deities, the palace, and so on, are like a magical illusion. This was the training in the 'deities who are the supported.'

The 'samaya deities' means the central figure surrounded by the other forms of Tara, which you have visualized. The palace is the support; it supports the deities. Imagine that each of the deities, both the central figure and the entire retinue, have certain syllables at their forehead, throat and heart centers—a white OM, a red AH, and a blue HUNG. The central figure and all the surrounding ones shine with rays of light emanating from these syllables. Then, these rays of light that are being sent out in boundless numbers invoke a replica of the whole mandala from the pure land of Tara. These deities are the 'wisdom deities' and they come, so the wisdom mandala can dissolve into the samaya mandala. Imagine that the two mandalas become indivisible. You repeat four syllables, DZA HUNG BAM HO, through which the wisdom deities become indivisible from you.

In some of the more elaborate tantric sadhanas, you also invoke the protection circle from the pure realm. Then you let it dissolve into the protection circle that you have visualized. The palace arrives and dissolves into the palace. In this case, the chief figure dissolves into the chief figure and the remaining deities dissolve into their particular representations. That is known as 'sealing.'

Next comes the empowering aspect. From your heart center, send out rays of light that invoke the empowerment deities of the five families. They carry vases of nectar with which they empower you, pouring it down through the top of your head into your whole body, so that each inch is filled with nectar that purifies all defilements. The remnants of the nectar overflowing from above turn into the lord of the family—in this case, Buddha Amitabha. He is wearing the attire of a nirmanakaya buddha. You are similarly crowned to be a buddha.[23]

From your own heart center, you now send out offering goddesses that fill the expanse of the sky and make offerings to you. There are eight offering goddesses, each carrying their various offerings and singing *The Royal Tantra of Praises* in very melodious voices. After a while, these goddesses dissolve into you. You can repeat this by emanating more offering goddesses, who make offerings and sing praises. Again, they dissolve into you. Continue to emanate the offerings and praises again and again, until you get tired of it. This helps to clarify the complete mandala and all the deities. This was the first aspect of achieving some steadiness in the samadhi of the mandala and the deities.

It is important when going through a sadhana text to do so systematically, paying careful attention to all the details. Begin by developing the visualization. Then go through the process of invoking the deities, dissolving the wisdom beings into samaya beings, requesting them to take a seat, and making offerings and praises. Normally the recitation of mantra comes next. However, it is the original tradition to not jump immediately into reciting the mantra, but to relax a bit and allow all the details to come to mind, starting from the beginning. To do this, you simply recall what the protection circle looks like—the pure land inside it, the celestial palace in the middle of the pure land, the deities inside the celestial palace, the throne with the central figure, and the seed syllable in the heart center inside the central figure. Then go through it all again in the opposite direction, starting with the seed syllable inside the heart center of the central figure, the central figure, the surrounding deities, the palace, the pure land outside the palace, and the protection circle. You recall one feature after the other in a very serene and unperturbed way.

Then you do it starting from the bottom: first there is the vajra cross, and on top of that there are the layers of the five elements, Mount Meru, the celestial palace, the throne, and the central figure, with its legs, torso, and head, all the way up to the crown where Buddha Amitabha sits. Do this again in reverse order, visualizing from the top down to the bottom. Keep going through it repeatedly, as long as you enjoy doing this. All this still belongs to the first aspect of the sadhana, the body aspect, which must be carried out before going on to the speech aspect.

Jamgön Kongtrül instructs us to continue refreshing the vividness in this way until we are weary of it. This facet of the practice has three aspects: vivid features, which means all the details; stable pride, which is confidence that one is actually the deity; and pure symbolism. All three should be included here. That is the original intent in the tantras. Even though some people skip this aspect does not negate the fact that it is meant to be practiced in this fashion. In fact, it is a necessary component of sadhana practice. This is how they practice in the Sakya tradition. In addition, in the Chakrasamvara and Mahakala main practices, this is still necessary and included at the point before the recitation.

Recitation

Once you grow weary of bringing to mind the vividness of each feature, embark on the recitation part. Imagine that in the heart center of Arya Tara is a little lotus flower with a moon disc, upon which is the syllable TAM. Around that is coiled the ten-syllable Tara mantra, like a garland of mantra syllables, shining like the purest emeralds. They are situated in clockwise fashion, and glow with brilliant light.

Focus on these syllables. By doing so, they start to radiate even further. The syllable in the center and each syllable of the mantra garland send out innumerable tiny replicas of Tara in rays of light that fill the entire expanse of space. Everywhere is completely filled with forms of Tara and light rays that carry out the twelve deeds of the Buddha. They fulfill the twofold purpose by removing the obscurations and habitual tendencies of all sentient beings throughout the infinite expanse of the sky. Everyone is purified, turned into Tara themselves and established at the level of Tara's enlightenment.

These rays of light come back and dissolve into you. Because of this, you feel the confidence that you have now attained mastery over the four activities, the ten great siddhis, which are included in the common siddhis, and the supreme siddhi of Mahamudra. You imagine that you are fully accomplished. With this confidence, you recite the ten-syllable mantra of Tara in a way that is flawless and uninterrupted. Your attention does not stray towards anything else; you simply sustain one-pointed concentration by focusing on the deity, the mantra, and the emanating and re-absorbing of rays of light while chanting the mantra.

Regardless of what takes place here—in the visualization, the recitation, throughout all of this—understand that in no way is any of this other than the natural expression of the emptiness of your own mind. Everything that manifests is the self-display of emptiness. In other words, it has no concrete existence whatsoever, no solidity. In this way, you never part from the view of fully understanding that your nature is the unity of cognizant emptiness. This is a crucial point.

Having completed the number of recitations for the session, repeat the offerings and praises. Then you could simply say a specific mantra to request accomplishment, or you can spell it out as it is done here:

Bhagavati Arya Tara and your retinue,
Bestow upon me all attainments, common and supreme,
Both presently and ultimately
To dispel every type of fear.

With that, you partake of the nectar of accomplishment. Then you repeat the mantras for making up for faults and asking for forgiveness. Next, you ask the wisdom beings to depart, and you dissolve the samaya mandala into the state of luminous wakefulness. After a while, you again re-emerge in the form of a magical illusion as the body of Tara. Dedicate the merit, and utter the verses of aspirations and auspiciousness. Whether you practice according to number or according to fixed time, this is the way to practice a sadhana from beginning to end. This is the structure.

If you like, you could add a front visualization, which means a complete extra mandala in front. If you do a specific extended sadhana, there is no fixed timespan or fixed number. You have a front visualization, you make additional offerings on the shrine, and so forth. You still visualize yourself as the deity. There is an exchange of blessings and rays of light between the deity in front and you. You use the same sequence as before, but you make the offerings and praises even more lavishly. At the end of a set number of recitations, you invoke and receive the blessings of accomplishment, and receive the empowerments from the front visualization. This completes the stages for practicing the receiving of the wisdom blessings within your stream of being.

Once you have completed the primary recitation, which is the ten-syllable Tara mantra, OM TARE TUTTARE TURE SOHA, there is another mantra recitation for the whole retinue. The visualization is that the rays of light radiate from the heart center of the central figure and touch each of the Taras in the retinue, starting with the first eight and continuing on through the others. This invokes their minds so that each one is inspired to send out replicas of herself along with rays of light in countless number. These dispel hindrances for oneself and all others. The hindrances are due to anxieties and fears of the external types such as fire, water, and so on, and the eight inner fears related to emotional states, which include the five poisons, stinginess, doubt and wrong views. All of these are totally removed. They also bring forth whatever is desired, both presently and ultimately, like a wish-fulfilling jewel.

The number of recitations is ten times 100,000—one million of the primary mantra, then 40,000 of the mantra for the retinue. That is the proportion: one million of the primary to 40,000 of the retinue mantras. This is in terms of number, but if you are practicing in terms of time, Jamgön Kongtrül explains that by exerting yourself in this for three weeks, you will dispel hindrances, obstacles will be pacified and everything perfect will be increased. By practicing one-pointedly, you will accomplish the nondual profound brilliance, the ultimate realization. These are the benefits that are mentioned.

If a practitioner prefers a more concise practice than this, know that it is the tradition to first complete the full number of recitations in retreat before you consider doing a condensed daily practice.

Sadhana Retreat

I will now explain how to structure a retreat on this practice. First of all, you should always start a longer retreat during the waning part of the lunar calendar, beginning near the end of the day. You should of course have received any empowerments required for the retreat. If you have received the empowerment and not done the practice or kept the recitation alive, some damage to the samayas may have occurred. Therefore, it is recommended and sometimes necessary to request the empowerment right before beginning retreat and receive it one more time, so that it's fresh.

Traditionally, in a recitation retreat there are four sessions each day. The first session is during the time that lies in between the first light in the sky—the break of day—until the sun rises above the horizon. The second session takes place after sunrise until midday. The third session is between midday and sunset, while the fourth session is between sunset and darkness, also called the dusk session This general system does not say how long each session should be—tradition simply states that there should be four. Some could be longer and some shorter, according to your preference. If the sadhana text is very long, so that you feel that you cannot do more than three sessions, the one to eliminate is the dusk session.

Now, here is how to practice during the four sessions. During the first one, the dawn session, go through all the steps that were mentioned as the preliminary parts: the reflections that belong to renunciation and guru devotion. Train yourself as well in the teachings that in this text correspond to the person of the lesser and medium capacity—the four mind-changings, refuge, bodhichitta, and so forth. These can be done by bringing each to mind sequentially.

In the second session, you are allowed to go through all of them again, just very fast. It is not required to go through them again because you are in retreat and have already gone through them once. Thus, in the second session you could begin with refuge and bodhichitta and carry on through to the recitation, and so forth. At the end of the afternoon session, you should add the petition to the Dharma protectors. Do that in addition to making any torma offerings, dissolving and emerging. Do not do this portion after the sun has set, or at nighttime. Some texts have a petition to the Dharma protectors within the sadhana text, but this does not mean you have to do it in each session—you can do it during the third one.

During recitation retreat, there are certain times when you should not have a recitation session, such as exactly at midnight and exactly at noon. Likewise, when the sun first appears over the horizon and as it sets are times when negative forces roam about rampantly. This holds true for tummo practice as well—these times should be avoided.

During a sadhana retreat with recitation, it is traditional to decide beforehand how many mantras to repeat during each session. It is not a matter of doing whatever you feel like, deciding that, "Oh well, today I will do more, because it is interesting"—and then the next day you do less because you are busy. If you have drawn up a program beforehand, it is important to stick to it. If you decide to do 2,000 or 4,000, fulfill your commitment, and don't do less or more than that. The total does not have to be the same number for each session within a day, but it's important to keep the same totals that you have decided for each session. You could do more recitations in the first and fourth sessions, say, and less in the two middle ones. Arrange it any way you like, but make sure each day follows the same patterns. In the Drukpa Kagyü tradition of Yamantaka, Vajrasattva and guru yoga, it is said that one should keep the same routine from day to day

Jamgön Kongtrül also says to "chant in a flawless way," which means that while reciting, you should not let your thoughts wander. You need to maintain one-pointed mindfulness. It is taught that if you have reached a quarter of the way around and suddenly you feel overcome by drowsiness, you need to start from the beginning of that rosary again. It is not that you sneeze or cough or yawn and merely carry on. If you want to give in to that, you start over from the beginning of that rosary. It is also said that if you find out that you have been thinking about something totally unrelated to the practice, as soon as you notice it, start from the beginning once more. Don't continue reciting while thinking of something totally unrelated. This is actually a skillful instruction, since it causes you to stick to the practice rather than being distracted.

Moreover, you should always divide the number of recitations into three parts. One-third should be 'body recitation,' bringing to mind the vivid features of the mandala, the deity, the retinue, and so forth. In this part, you train in vivid presence, stable pride and pure symbolism.

While your voice recites the mantra, you recall all the features distinctly and in very detailed fashion. The second third is devoted to 'speech recitation.' Whatever the sadhana text says, like "the rays of light accomplish…," you imagine that it happens. While emanating and reabsorbing, obtaining the siddhis, we accomplish the welfare of sentient of beings. While reciting, you imagine that all of this happens. The third portion is the 'mind recitation,' in which you simply sustain the continuity of original wakefulness, which is the mind of the deity. Recite the mantra while maintaining the ongoing state of rigpa. You always divide up the recitation session into three equal portions for body, speech and mind. This is the general method of the new and the old schools, Sarma and Nyingma both.

There are four aspects to the recitation itself: approach, full approach, accomplishment and great accomplishment. The approach is called 'the moon with a garland of stars.' Here, you simply focus your attention on the seed syllable in the heart center, surrounded by the other syllables of the mantra. Just keep your mind on that while reciting. For the full approach, the second aspect, the garland begins to spin in a circle like a 'revolving firebrand.' The image comes from swinging a burning stick at nighttime. The third, the accomplishment, known as 'the messenger of the king,' begins with the emanation of light rays. If there are male and female figures, the garland will extend from the heart center and down through the male vajra into the female's lotus, then up to her heart center, out of her mouth, and into the male's mouth. The fourth recitation aspect is the great accomplishment. In this, all the syllables resound with their own sound simultaneously, while each of the deities send out replicas of themselves from their heart centers, including mantras and rays of light. The image for this is 'a beehive breaking open,' filling the whole universe with the mantra recitation and deities.

An alternative image for the third aspect, accomplishment, is that the main deity is like a king or queen, and all the activities are carried out like emissaries being sent out in all directions to pacify, increase, magnetize and subjugate.

There are three traditional indicators for how long the retreat should last: fixed timespan, fixed numbers, and the sign of accomplishment—time, number and sign. For fixed timespan, six months is mentioned in all the tantras as a sufficient period. In terms of numbers, it is usually said that 400,000 or 700,000 mantras are a bare minimum. The general rule is to multiply the number of syllables in the mantra by 100,000. If it has ten syllables, the total should be ten times 100,000, which is one million. That is the common rule of thumb.

After the passing of Buddha Shakyamuni, each period becomes more and more degenerate. We are presently in the age of strife, so the formula should be 400,000 for each syllable, simply to make up for the negativity of the present age. The number mentioned here in the text is ten times 100,000. That makes one million, which is the recitation measure. If you do a major recitation, it will be four times that because we are in the age of strife. Therefore, it would be four million.

In addition, there is something called the mending number, which is always one-tenth. For example if you have chanted 100,000, the mending would be 10,000. This is to make up for anything you might have miscounted or forgotten. In addition to that, when your recitation session is about to finish, before ending, recite the Ali-Kali, the vowel-consonant mantra, three times. This makes up for any mispronunciations, omissions or faults. Then there is the Essence of Causation mantra to stabilize the blessings of the recitation. In addition, repeat the hundred-syllable Vajrasattva mantra three times to apologize for any mistakes or distraction.

Now about the sign: this can occur either in actuality, in a vision, or in dream. It needs to be one of the three. Actuality means in an awake state, where one is not sleeping. If there is some sign of having attained accomplishment, immediately receive the blessings, meaning that you take accomplishment from the nectar on the shrine, the nectar that has been kept there as the substance of accomplishment. Imagine that from the secret space of the male and female deities, rays of light go to all the buddhas, come back, and dissolve into the nectar that you partake of without delay. If you wait too long, there is a risk that the substance of accomplishment could either dissipate or be stolen by some spirit. It is perfectly all right, each time you have a certain sign or indication in a dream, to take the blessings from the shrine in the morning. You can do this many times; in fact, it is even better like that.

There is also a subsequent fire puja, which involves extra recitations of one-tenth the total number. The specifics depend on what kind of sadhana you have been doing, but the general way of mending a number of recitations is to use the pacifying activity, even though you could be going into the four activities. In a particular setting, build a fire, then add certain ingredients into the fire while reciting. In addition, there are here extra syllables to put at the end of the mantra. It is definitely the tradition to conclude a major recitation retreat with a fire puja.

There is no meddling with the set number of recitations you are to do in a retreat. However, when you have finished retreat and come out, do one-tenth extra with a fire puja. If you think this is too difficult, then you are allowed to call upon other Dharma friends to come practice the fire puja together with you, counting the number of recitations of each person and adding them all together.

Anuttara Yoga

We now come to the third section of the text, the Anuttara Yoga, where there are both the special preliminaries and the yoga of the main part.

Special Preliminaries

For the special preliminaries, the refuge and bodhichitta are the same as previously explained. However, instead of Vajrasattva, there is the vajra samaya recitation and meditation, in which Amoghasiddhi is invoked to purify our negative karma and obscurations. To do that, imagine that you are seated in your ordinary form, and that at the crown of your head is a white lotus flower with a moon disc atop it. Upon the lotus sits your root guru in the form of Amoghasiddhi, green in color, holding a sword in one hand and a bell in the other. He is seated in union with his own consort, Samaya Tara. They are dressed in silks, jewels and bone ornaments, fully ablaze with all the major and minor marks, and seated in a cross-legged posture. In Amoghasiddhi's heart center, upon a moon disc, is the syllable HA, surrounded by his mantra. The syllables of the mantra chain send out rays of light that make offerings to all noble beings and purify sentient beings' obscurations. Returning back, the rays turn into a stream of nectar that flows down, entering the opening at the top of your head. It flows into and fills your body, purifying illness, evil influences, negative karma and obscurations, and increasing the original wakefulness of great bliss. With this in mind, recite one-pointedly the mantra of Amoghasiddhi and consort with the extra lines for removing negative karma and obscurations.

Recite the Amoghasiddhi mantra 100,000 times, or until the sign of having purified negative karma has occurred. When ready to finish the session, chant the verse according to the general way of concluding the purification, with "Protector, through my ignorance," and so forth. Imagine that this bestows the absolution. Then your guru in the form of Amoghasiddhi melts into light and dissolves into you. Feeling confident that this is the case, simply rest in the equanimity of your original, natural state. This is part of the special preliminaries for the practice.

The next part is based on guru yoga, and its purpose is to gather the accumulations and receive the blessings. First, visualize the support by uttering the following:

"AH, in the sky before me, within the sphere of five-colored light, on a white lotus and a full moon disc, sits my guru in the form of green Arya Tara. Her hand is in the gesture of supreme giving, holding the utpala lotus. She wears silks and jewel ornaments and is peacefully smiling, ablaze with the resplendent major and minor marks. She is the single embodiment of the Three Precious Ones. She emanates oceanlike cloudbanks of the Three Roots, and is vividly present as the nature of utter perfection."

Then pick up the mandala offering plate and place either seven or thirty-seven heaps on it, offering them in accordance with the general tradition. Say the following lines for the mandala offering, repeated as many times as you are able:

OM AH HUNG⁏

The three realms, vessel and contents, glory and riches,⁏
My body, luxuries and all virtues,⁏
I offer to the lords of compassion.⁏
Accepting them, please bestow your blessings.⁏
OM SARVA TATHAGATA RATNA MANDALA PUJA HOH⁏

Now for the supplication, with deepfelt and intense devotion say the lines beginning, "Kye, kye Lama Jetsünma," and so forth. This means, "Hear me, guru Arya Tara. From my heart, I sincerely call upon you. Bestow your blessings, dispel obstacles, and give me the four empowerments and all the siddhis." Recite this supplication with its specific mantra one hundred or one thousand times, or as many times as you can. At the end, imagine that you receive the four empowerments while saying these lines:

> From my guru Arya Tara's forehead
> The white OM radiates light that dissolves into my own
>   forehead,
> Through which I receive the vase empowerment
> That purifies the karmic actions of my body.
> It empowers me to practice the development stage as
>   the path.
> As a result, I am installed with the fortune to attain
>   nirmanakaya.
>
> From the red AH in her throat, rays of light emanate.
> They dissolve into my own throat.
> I obtain the secret empowerment that purifies the
>   defilements of my voice
> And empowers me to practice the path of channels and
>   energies.

As a result, I am invested with the fortune to attain
sambhogakaya.

From the HUNG in her heart center, blue rays of light
shine out,
Dissolving into my own heart center.
I obtain the wisdom-knowledge empowerment
That purifies the mental obscurations
And empowers me to practice the phonya path.
As a result, I am invested with the fortune to attain
dharmakaya.

Once again from all three places, white, red and blue
rays of light radiate.
Dissolving into my three places, I obtain the fourth
empowerment.
It purifies the defilement for wisdom and empowers me
To train in the path of the Great Perfection.
As a result, I am invested with the fortune to attain the
svabhavikakaya.

Having spoken these lines and received the empowerments, say then: "Due to even greater deepfelt devotion, the
guru Arya Tara melts into light and dissolves into me. Her
three secrets—body, speech and mind—and my own three
doors become of the same taste." Imagining this, "I remain
composed for as long as possible in the original nature of
luminous wakefulness, while sustaining the natural state of
my mind."

This completes the special preliminaries.

The Main Part

The main part refers to the secret great accomplishment and has four aspects that will be explained one after the other, in a successive way. The first is the Initial Yoga, second is the Subsequent Yoga, third the Exquisite Yoga, and fourth the Great Yoga. Each has a specific explanation.

The Initial Yoga—Visualization

The Initial Yoga has three practices: visualization, recitation and completion. First comes the visualization of the samaya mandala, starting with unfolding the structure of the three samadhis as the cause, and the deities as the result. These three samadhis were not explained earlier. That is one of the main differences between this and the previous levels of sadhana practice [below Anuttara Yoga].

The first of the three samadhis corresponds to the view that you trained in previously, the view of emptiness that is ultimate bodhichitta. Here you keep the assurance that all phenomena—the world and sentient beings, whatever you experience, all that may appear and live—have from the very beginning never come into existence. They are emptiness that never arises. This emptiness totally defies any limiting conceptual constructs that one may have, just like wide-open space. Training in this frame of mind is the first of the three samadhis, called 'samadhi of suchness,' which means great emptiness.

For the second, the state of ultimate bodhichitta, you allow the compassionate training to be manifested by thinking in the following way: "This natural state is not understood by sentient beings. They do not realize it.

Because of that, and from no actual basis whatsoever, they deludedly invent all the thought constructs about what is. This occurs from moment to moment, in an endless stream of samsara that creates unbearable suffering. How incredibly sad!" That kind of compassion is the second of the three samadhis, called the 'samadhi of illumination' in which compassion is like a magical illusion.

The third samadhi is the unity of emptiness and compassion that naturally expresses itself as the syllable TAM. Radiant in the midst of space, it appears like a rainbow in the sky—visible in a single instant. It is vivid, brilliant. This is the 'samadhi of the seed syllable,' which is the source of everything. These three samadhis are the opening of a sadhana practice on this level, and are known as the causal practice.

Now comes the resultant practice, which entails the support and the supported, the mandala and the deities. From the syllable TAM, the syllables for the wisdom fire, wind, and water appear. From these, the world and beings, the ideas of concreteness we may have, are all utterly burned, blown and flushed away, so that everything becomes emptiness. The syllable TAM then sends out rays of light, creating the vajra ground with the fence, dome, and latticework, outside of which is the blazing wisdom fire. Within this protection circle, the syllable TAM emanates the syllable DHRUNG of multicolored light, which transforms itself into a celestial palace of five types of jewels and of unfathomable proportions. It has four sides, four gates, four portals, and is exquisite in all its ornaments and decorations, which symbolize in both form and meaning the thirty-seven aspects of the path to enlightenment. These characteristics of the celestial palace are all fully complete. Within the center of this palace, there is an eight-petalled lotus flower, in the center of which are anthers and pistils. Moon discs rest on the petals in the four cardinal directions, while sun discs are on the petals at the four gates. Bringing these to mind one after the other is called the 'mandala of the support.'

At this point, we imagine that in the central area of the celestial palace is a moon disc, curving slightly upward, with a sun disc below it. Together, they form a completely closed sphere. The syllable TAM enters and lands inside this sun-moon sphere, transforming into a green utpala flower marked with TAM in the center. This TAM syllable emanates rays of light, making offerings to all the conquerors and their offspring, and purifying the negative emotions and karma of all sentient beings, establishing them at the level of Tara.

The light returns back and I transform into the buddha Samaya Tara, of green color, peacefully smiling, with a compassionate and lovely countenance. My shiny black hair is arranged on top of my head. Half is tied up into a peak with a wish-fulfilling jewel, while the rest flows freely down my back. 'My' left hand is extended in the gesture of supreme giving. The right hand is at the heart center. In holds in the gesture of bestowing protection, between the thumb and the ring finger, the stem of the utpala flower that blooms at the level of my ear with a fully opened lotus blossom. My right leg is extended in a majestic pose. I am seated, and on my lap is the consort who is my natural radiance, in the form of Dorje Tachok, which means Supreme Vajra Steed. He is a particular form of Amoghasiddhi, and has a slightly wrathful and passionate expression. Holding a sword and a bell in his hands, he embraces me as Tara. Both the male and female figures are visualized as wearing the upper garment, the lower garment, and the jewel and bone ornaments.

The Sambhogakaya Attire

When receiving instructions on Vajrasattva practice in the context of the early preliminary practices, you were doubtless taught the sambhogakaya attire of the five silken garments and the eight jewel ornaments. All sambhogakaya buddhas, whether male or female, wear the same basic attire and ornaments. Having received the instructions of the Vajrasattva practice, you should be familiar with this attire. However, I would like to go through it one more time to make sure that you know what Tara is wearing.

The first of the five silken garments of Tara's apparel is a big shawl that falls over her shoulders, extending in both directions, and tied at several places as it flows downward. The second are the leggings, which are very loose, of red color, and tied together at the waist and at the ankles. The third is the skirt, which ties around the waist and is flowing. It falls outside the pants and has very special ornaments on it. It is rainbow-colored, made of five types of material sewn together. When you look at drawings of the sambhogakaya deity, it looks as if the skirt is part of the leggings, but actually it is another piece of billowing silk that drapes the body below the shawl. The fourth is a silken scarf that goes under the tiara, like a headband, and flows down beside each shoulder. The fifth is ribbons that flow down her hair and back, all the way down to her waist. Some of the layers continue all the way down to her ankles. These are the five main silken garments.

Tara's hair is bound up into two equal portions. In this case, the ties are in three segments, so that a red band intersects each level. At the top of her head is a wish-fulfilling jewel. That is according to most traditions. Some traditions depict the hair differently, with only two pieces, with two buns on each side. Here there are three pieces pulled up, with the rest of the hair flowing down her back all the way down to her waist.

All sambhogakaya buddhas wear the eight jewel ornaments. First is the crown, with five segments of jewels. Second are the earrings, big ornamented hoops studded with jewels. There are two basic designs, depending on which way they are turning, with large circular segments hanging. Third is the choker, a short necklace that is filigreed with many jewels. After that is the longer necklace that goes over the breast, and the longest necklace that reaches all the way down to the navel. There is also a belt, beautifully filigreed and jeweled, that encircles her body. There are upper armlets and wrist bracelets. Finally, there are anklets. Altogether, that makes eight; together with the five silken ornaments, these constitute the thirteenfold attire of the sambhogakaya buddha.

There are also bone ornaments that are not usually mentioned at the time of introducing the simple form of Vajrasattva. That is to make it easier for beginners. It simplifies the general peaceful deity practice, for instance, of Tara, Amitayus, the peaceful mandala deities, and so forth. However, at this level of practice you should visualize the deity wearing latticework ornaments made of bone. There are two oral traditions explaining what these look like. One tells of bone latticework interwoven with jewels and studded with gemstones. The other describes the bone latticework as being next to the skin and the jewelry on top of that, in layers.

The Retinue

Next you visualize the deities in the retinue, who emerge from the male and female's union. From their secret space, TAM DHRUNG HRIH HUNG—four white, yellow, red and black syllables that are the nature of awakened mind—fly out into the four directions, each landing on its own seat. Each one emanates rays of light that return back, similar to the earlier visualization of making offerings to benefit beings. Each syllable is transformed into a particular form of Tara. To the east, in front, is Vajra Tara, who is blue and has a peaceful expression. In her left hand, she holds a blue lotus marked with a vajra. To the south, which is to Tara's right, is Ratna Tara, of yellow color and with a playful expression, holding in her left hand a yellow utpala flower marked with a jewel. To the west is Padma Tara, red in color, with a passionate expression. In her left hand she holds a red lotus marked with a hook. To the north, behind the main figure, is Karma Tara, black in color, with a wrathful expression. In her left hand, she holds a black utpala flower marked with a sword. All four of them hold their right hand in the gesture of supreme giving. They all wear silken and jeweled ornaments, and are seated in a half-open, crossed-legged position.

Now again from the place of union of the central figure, from the bodhichitta, the four syllables DZA HUNG BAM HO fly out, one into each of the four directions and land at the four gates of the palace. Here one turns into the white Hook Tara, who in her right hand holds a hook. At the south gate the syllable transforms into Shackle Tara, who is yellow and holds shackles in her right hand. To the west is the Chain Tara, who is red and holds chains in her right hand. Finally, to the north is the Bell Tara, who is green and holds a bell in her right hand. All four of them hold an utpala in their left hand. All are peaceful and smiling, yet with a wrathful expression at the same time. The first set of four Taras were the four families and were sitting down, but the Taras at the four gates are dancing, one leg straight and the other raised. They are also wearing silk and jewel ornaments.

The central figure and the retinue are all present within a sphere of radiant wisdom light, the natural radiance of their own original wakefulness. At the level of their foreheads, they have a white OM, at their throats a red AH, and at the heart centers a blue HUNG. These syllables are indivisible in identity from the three vajras of body, speech and mind of all buddhas. This is how you should visualize. In some sadhanas, it says that at the forehead, throat and heart there is, respectively, a lotus flower, moon, and vajra, inside of which are respectively the three syllables OM AH HUNG. This detail is not mentioned here, so you can simply visualize the three syllables.

Vivid Presence

The experiences and perceptions of an ordinary world and ordinary sentient beings are called the 'basis for purification.' That which purifies is the training in the complete mandala of the support and the supported. Through this, our clinging to ordinary perception is purified into the experience of being the deity, of a divine nature. This is how we lay the foundation for the extraordinary realization of the completion stage. All these procedures for visualization are accomplished by our possessing in completeness the three principles of vivid presence, stable pride and pure recollection.

Begin the training in vivid presence by gathering the accumulations. Follow through into the main part of the sadhana by visualizing the samaya mandala, inviting and dissolving the wisdom circle, paying homage, making offerings, praises, and so forth. Do not merely read the words out loud. For each section of a sadhana, vivid presence should be brought forth in your mind. Experience this distinctness from the top of the head of the central figure down to the base of the throne. Bring to mind as clearly as you can the face, hands, arms, color, ornaments, the attire and the facial expression of the main figure. At the end, the complete bodily form can be perceived in a brilliant way.

Once you have accomplished the vivid presence of the central figure, proceed to the surrounding deities, one after the other. Continue with visualizing the celestial palace, the surroundings, and the pure land outside the celestial palace. Next, envision the protection circle of vajras with the flames of fire. Each detail is pictured mentally, one after the other. Sometimes you begin with the external celestial palace, the surrounding deities, and then the chief figure, moving gradually from outside to inside. No matter how you do this, bring to mind the distinct features of the mandala and the deities. Avoid giving in to dullness, drowsiness, agitation, or absentmindedness. Instead, focus one-pointedly on the features to be cultivated, in an uninterrupted way. Begin with short periods, but repeat them many times. Gradually extend those periods until you are capable of continuing from the beginning to the end of the session with each feature appearing as clearly as a reflection on the surface of a clean mirror. On the surface of a mirror, it is possible for many images to appear simultaneously. According to this method, the support and the supported—meaning the entire mandala, the palace and deities—can appear in your mind in completeness. Remember, though, that they appear without any concrete nature, like the moon reflected in water, or like a rainbow appearing in the sky, vividly and brilliantly. That is how you should train in experiencing the vivid presence.

Stable Pride

Stable pride also needs to be developed. The support and the supported, whatever is visualized, are in actuality identical to the ultimate fruition. In other words, this is the fully perfect result, right here, right now. Train in having that kind of assurance, perfecting the pride in whatever you visualize, whatever you form in your mind. Know that it is never separate from its nature, which is the meaning of equal taste. By generating this stable pride, we overcome the ordinary concepts of clinging to a self that is based on the aggregates, the elements, a personal name or the like. Instead, everything refers to the bodily form and nature of the deity.

Regardless of whether or not the visualization is completely clear, you should still generate the feeling that "I am in actuality, since the very beginning, fully endowed with the enlightened body, speech, mind, qualities and activities of Noble Samaya Tara, the mother who gives birth to all the buddhas." As well, have the attitude that "I am the single identity that embodies the activity of the three mysteries of all conquerors and their offspring." Generate this kind of self-confidence not in an artificial way, but by training until it becomes totally sincere and genuine, and you are thereby able to turn away from clinging to being an ordinary person.

Pure Recollection

The third principle is pure recollection, and it has two aspects: symbolic purity and true purity. Symbolic purity is as follows: The single face of Tara symbolizes that all phenomena are of one taste, which is suchness. The two arms are the unity of means and knowledge, prajña and *upaya*. The extended right leg means not dwelling in the extreme of passive nirvana, while the bent left leg represents transcending samsaric existence. Because she manifests as the chief figure of the all-accomplishing wisdom family, her bodily form is of green color.

She has a peacefully smiling, compassionate expression, symbolizing her loving passion for sentient beings. Her right hand is in the gesture of supreme giving, symbolizing the bestowal of siddhi to the practitioner, or to anyone who wants to practice this. The left is in the gesture of giving protection, which symbolizes bestowing fearlessness to sentient beings. She holds the blue utpala flower, which symbolizes her unimpeded activity.

The hair tied up on the top of her head with the remnant flowing freely down her back symbolizes that all virtuous qualities are fully perfected as well as her acceptance of other beings. The silken garments and leggings symbolize being utterly liberated from the torment of negative emotions. The jewel ornaments represent wearing the wisdoms as adornment, without rejecting sense-pleasures. The bone ornaments of the six types symbolize having fully perfected the six paramitas. Being in union with the consort Supreme Vajra Steed symbolizes the unity of skillful means as great bliss, indivisible from the manifest aspect of wisdom that is utterly unchanging.

The four goddesses, Tara's radiance, are the retinue, symbolizing the other four wisdoms. The four Taras at the gates, the gatekeepers, symbolize the spontaneous fulfillment of the four activities. The celestial palace symbolizes the thirty-seven features of the path to enlightenment— sign, meaning, and symbol are here in manifest form. The indestructible vajra enclosure symbolizes being uninterrupted by conceptual thoughts. The fire outside, surrounding everything, symbolizes having utterly defeated habitual tendencies of thought constructs. In this way, when bringing each of these aspects to mind, recollect their meaning. As well, this kind of practice has the ability to reverse the clinging to all ordinary perceptions.

In the oral tradition, it is taught that if one is not able to bring to mind all these features, one should at least remember their pure symbolism, one after the other. Then bring everything together in one attitude. To do this, acknowledge that the celestial palace, the buddhafield, Tara, and the whole mandala are the dharmakaya wisdom of all the buddhas and the inconceivable qualities, manifesting out of wondrous compassion. In order to symbolize all the qualities of wisdom, compassion, and so forth, it has taken this particular form. For a beginner, training in that kind of devotion will suffice as a resemblance of the true and vast recollection of purity.

Do not think there is something superior to the deity that you are visualizing, as in, "Well, I am doing this but there is still something other that is better." That is not stable pride. The stable pride of identifying with Tara is to know that your nature is indivisible from prajñaparamita, which is the ultimate Tara.

The true recollection of purity is as follows: the entire mandala that we have trained in above is not to be regarded as having material and concrete existence. You should also be totally free of any clinging to an ordinary feeling of being yourself. Being unfettered by the ordinary way of perceiving means that everything you experience is devoid of any concrete nature. It is completely insubstantial. Think, "It is my mind, which is empty, that appears in the form of the deity. The deity is in identity my own empty mind, and has no existence apart from my own mind. In this way, appearance and emptiness are of one single nature." Understand this. It corresponds to the statement in *The Heart Sutra*: "Form is emptiness, emptiness is form; form is no other than emptiness, emptiness is no other than form."

In this way, the development stage makes use of these three features—vivid presence, stable pride and pure recollection—to attain accomplishment. By training in these three for an extended period, you will gradually achieve a vividness of mind in 'the three fields,' with regard to the threefold level of objects. Eventually you will obtain the four measures of clarity and the four measures of stability in a full-fledged way.[24] This brings an end to clinging to ordinary perceptions and is the highest phase of accomplishment, at which point you have reached the final level of the development stage.

Recitation

The second point is the recitation. It corresponds with the causes for vajra speech and has the purpose to purify the defilements of the three doors. We should understand that the 'mantra deity' arises from the recitation of mantra, and the wisdom deity is the result of accomplishing the mantra as a cause. Consequently, you become closer and closer to realizing the wisdom deity by means of the mantra. It is said, "Fan the fire-like development stage with the wind-like recitation." In this way, you will swiftly bring forth the power of the meditation practice. I would like to stress that it is the nature of things that the recitation brings forth the power of realizing the deity.

This recitation itself has five segments, one for each of enlightened body, speech, mind, qualities and activities. Here is the explanation for each recitation. First is the body recitation, which purifies defilements. Imagine yourself in the form of Samaya Tara, in whose heart center is the wisdom being, the dark blue Vajra Varahi. The wisdom being is holding a curved knife and skull cup filled with blood, and is dancing majestically in an upright posture upon a lotus and sun disc. In her heart center is a sphere made of a joined sun and moon, within which is the samadhi being, the green syllable TAM. The mantra garland to be recited surrounds it. The light rays shining from the garland are as brilliant as the morning sun striking a pure crystal. They radiate out, filling up the entire interior of your body with an unimpeded light that instantaneously purifies your being, in the same way that the rising sun immediately and totally eliminates all darkness. All the obscurations of the two types and all the habitual tendencies that have been created since beginningless time are completely eradicated in a single instant. While imagining this, one recites the body mantra.

The second aspect is the speech recitation, which causes the blessings to shower down. Using the same basis as the first recitation, the specific visualization now is that the garland of syllables of the mantra being recited sends out rays of light into the ten directions. These extend infinitely and turn into an inconceivable amount of offering clouds. These pleasing offerings are presented to the buddhas and bodhisattvas everywhere, who in return send back blessings of their body, speech and mind, the supreme and common siddhis. Their fivefold wisdom wealth appears in the form of lights and spheres that return and dissolve into you, so that you become indivisible from all these blessings. While imagining this, recite the speech mantra.

The third aspect is the mind recitation that incites or provokes great bliss. From the nada at the very tip of the TAM syllable in the heart center, the mantra chain emerges in an unceasing way, flowing out of the female deity's mouth into the mouth of the male deity. It moves down through his body to the secret vajra, and through it enters into the space of the female, where it rises and dissolves into the syllable in her heart center. The mantra chain continues like this uninterruptedly, like a whirling firebrand creating a stream of light. Circling in this way in the midstream of both the male and female deity, the wisdom of great bliss arises, so that the supreme, unchanging siddhi of Mahamudra is accomplished. Recite the mind mantra while keeping this in mind. The number of recitations for each of these three— body, speech and mind—is 100,000.

The fourth is the qualities recitation that fully perfects the mandala. The visualization is as follows: around the seed syllable, the specific mantra for qualities revolves as a garland. From the bodies of yourself and all the other deities in the mandala, replicas of your forms emerge in various sizes, from huge to tiny. From the jade garlands of the mantra appear mantra garlands and from the heart centers stream symbolic implements of each deity, as well as five-colored rays of light as innumerable as dust motes in a beam of sunlight. These all fill up the expanse of the sky. Imagine that all the mandalas of the Three Roots of the conquerors are pleased with these unexcelled offerings, and that all sentient beings of the three realms are purified of their two obscurations. Whatever appears, whatever is heard or thought of, is the play of deity, mantra, and original wakefulness. Everything then dissolves back into you. Imagining this, recite the mantra for qualities in a number that is four times 100,000.

The fifth recitation is of the activity that brings all activities to fulfillment. Having completed the set number for the four recitations above, imagine that from the forehead, throat, heart and navel of all the mandala deities appear light rays of white, red, blue and yellow, in countless numbers that utterly permeate the universe. Through this, the body, speech and mind of all sentient beings are protected from the eight major and sixteen other types of fear. The light rays spontaneously accomplish the four types of activity of pacifying, increasing, magnetizing and subjugating. While visualizing this, recite the *dharani* activity mantra 40,000 times. At the end of each session, repeat the offerings and praises, using *The Royal Tantra of Praises*.

Completion Stage

In order to dispel the limit of clinging to permanence during the stages of recitation, at the end of each session, dissolve everything into emptiness in the following way: The seed syllable in the heart center of the chief figure emanates rays of light, transforming the universe and beings into a pure mandala. All of that then gradually dissolves into the flames, the flames into the vajra enclosure, and that into the celestial palace, the mandala temple. The palace dissolves into the retinue of deities, which themselves dissolve into the central figure of Tara with male consort. The male dissolves into the female, and the female then begins to disappear, starting from the extremities, as the head and legs slowly vanish, and moving towards the center until only the seed syllable TAM is left. That too dissolves gradually from the bottom up, until only the fine nada tip, which is extremely subtle, is left. Keep your attention focused on that for a while, until at some point you dissolve even this, and settle evenly within the basic space of luminous wakefulness. Once again, in an instant, you reappear as the lucid unity that is the bodily form of the deity, like a magical illusion. You then carry on the practice in which all sights, sounds and thoughts are the play of the three mandalas of enlightened body, speech and mind. After completing this practice, dedicate the merit. This completes the first of the four yogas.

The Subsequent Yoga

A practitioner who has already brought forth the vivid presence of the previous development stage of the Initial Yoga can now embark on this yoga. About this second yoga, one tantra says,

> Abiding always in your heart
> Is a changeless, single sphere.
> The person who grows used to it
> Will surely feel the wakefulness.

This statement refers to the following: In order to bring forth the original wakefulness that has not yet arisen within your experience, or to stabilize it if it has, visualize the subtle spheres at the upper and lower extremities of the central channel. This refers to the meaning of AH and HUNG.

Even more profound than this is to focus the attention on the indestructible sphere in the center of the *dharmachakra*. For this, place the body in the cross-legged vajra posture, hands resting in fists on the thighs, back straight, and so on, according to the general description. Remain in a way in which the functioning of the five sense faculties is bound. The key point of mind is to focus on the sphere of light comprised of the five pure essences situated in the center of the heart. Visualize it as brilliantly clear, the size of a mustard seed or a pea. Direct the attention towards it exclusively, without being interrupted by any other thought. Keep simply this focus in mind, capturing the attention completely. This will gradually provoke all the signs of progress, such as the smoke-like sign and the others, which you experience one after the other.

Having grown steadily familiar with this, do not hold in mind even the shape of this tiny sphere in the heart center any longer. Instead, simply remain in the innate continuity of naturalness, your basic nature, without accepting or rejecting anything, without hope or fear, without projecting or concentrating. In other words, remain in and sustain the continuity of this state for as long as you can, without any mental activity whatsoever.

THE EXQUISITE YOGA

The third yoga is called 'the exquisite yoga' and has two parts: the actual and the enhancement.

The Actual Practice

Having attained stability in the samadhis described above, and having to some extent experienced original wakefulness, one should first do the training in the winds. Keep the sevenfold posture and exhale the stale breath. Until specific signs have occurred, continue counting the vajra recitation, training thoroughly in this prana path. Following that comes the four segments of prana practice with the vase-shaped breath, visualizing the four chakras. Continue in this until you reach a certain level of perfection.[25]

These preliminary steps are meant to bring your channels and winds to flexibility. Only after they become pliable is it possible to begin the practice of the *phonya* path, which is the actual practice. When that time has come, it is necessary to thoroughly train your own body as being the upaya. These days people, generally speaking, do not practice with another person's body; instead, they base the path of means on their own body while visualizing the consort.[26]

The yogi who has attained stability in the samadhi of undivided bliss and emptiness by growing accustomed to the practice using his or her own body can then practice the phonya path with another's body. To do this, first summon, examine, and bring the qualified consort to a certain level of insight. Begin by purifying their stream of being by teaching the expedient and definitive paths as the prelude. As the main part, gradually, as was indicated by the practice with your own body, practice and attain perfection.

Enhancement

The second part is the enhancement practice. After training in the path of unity—the threefold wisdom of bliss, warmth and nonthought—it is the intent of the tantras that you should accomplish the unity of the three kayas as fruition. You may have developed bliss through the previous path of means, but if the warmth has not been brought forth, you must take the support of the yoga of tummo.[27] At this point, there are specific yogic exercises to perform and apply as appropriate.

THE GREAT YOGA

The fourth yoga, called the Great Yoga, is an enhancement of nonthought. By doing a particular HUNG recitation and visualization, the samadhi of thoughtfree wakefulness as vast as the expanse of sky will spontaneously transcend center and edge, becoming utterly infinite. When that happens, dispense completely with the focus on prana practice, as well as any other kind of deliberate thought constructs.

Having suspended these, train in original, self-existing awareness. This self-existing awareness is utterly beyond constructs from the very beginning, and is by nature a lucid wakefulness. It is 'the fourth part without three,' the genuine, uncontrived and instantaneous wakefulness. Recognizing its identity, simply sustain its naturalness for as long as you can. Let all relative phenomena be brought to exhaustion within the inconceivable basic space of this ultimate nature. In this way, you reach the original ground of liberation. This concludes the fourth yoga.

CONCLUSION

Before presenting a few verses of poetry, Jamgön Kongtrül concludes his commentary of this gradual way for attaining realization based on Tara by describing how these practices are the entire path of gradual instructions that utterly perfect the supreme path of the four empowerments—that the skillful means of Vajrayana is extraordinary, enabling you to reach enlightenment within a single lifetime. If you are someone with devotion, perseverance, and pure samaya, and exert yourself in this practice, you will, by means of the 'indicating example wisdom,' before long fully realize the intrinsic great bliss that is 'indicated ultimate wisdom.' Tara is a manifestation of discriminating wisdom, the nature of which is luminous wakefulness. She is the heroine who swiftly carries out the activities of all the buddhas. She is the very identity of enlightened activity—beyond that which we can mentally imagine or fathom—and has incredible virtues that surpass any thought. Tara perfects all the inexhaustible adornment wheels that are the twenty-five attributes of fruition: five for body, five for speech, five for mind, five for qualities and five for activities. In short, through the symbolic meaning, you will realize the true state of original wakefulness. Within this very lifetime you will accomplish the state of the utterly indestructible, undefeatable and unchanging Vajra Tara of the innermost essence, who is prajñaparamita. Here is Jamgön Kongtrül's poetry:

> Look here, since from the treasury of mind, the vast
>   expanse of wisdom,
> I opened up a casket filled with priceless gems to enrich
>   all worthy students

Took a wish-fulfilling jewel, a deep instruction, never
known before,
And placed it at the summit of the banner of the noblest
of intents.

In order to fulfill the wish of both treasure masters,
To support the life of teaching-holders and expand their
noble deeds,
May the practice of this deepest teaching reach
perfection
So that siddhas of the two attainments can reach
everywhere throughout the world.

Jamgön Kongtrül ends his text by explaining that he
received these profound Tara teachings—both the ripening
empowerment and liberating instruction, personally and in
entirety—from the omniscient Dorje Ziji Tsal [another name
for Jamyang Khyentse Wangpo] when he was given a statue
so full of blessings that Khyentse considered it indivisible
from Tara. Having bestowed this great kindness, he also
gave Jamgön Kongtrül the command to propagate this
teaching through an appropriate clarification in writing.

A long time passed and the reason he let the time slip
by, Jamgön Kongtrül adds, was because this profound
instruction was a root text that combines both sutra and
tantra in words that are extremely profound and concise,
which should be elaborated upon fully and to do so would
require too much writing. However, presenting a brief
version would hardly be beneficial. When he reached the
age of seventy-eight, he kept bringing to mind the need to
accomplish his guru's command. Therefore, he took the
terma root text merely as the outline and wrote a teaching
in an appropriate length, neither too elaborate nor too short.

This he did at a site of great accomplishment, the retreat place known as Dzongshö Deshek Düpa while signing his name as 'the old *kusulu* Lodrö Taye.' May virtuous goodness increase.

This concludes the teaching on the guidance manual of Arya Tara entitled *The Essential Instruction on the Threefold Excellence*.

APPENDIX

A DESCRIPTION OF TARA BY THE 15TH GYALWANG KARMAPA

The venerable Arya Tara is the wisdom form of all the buddhas and bodhisattvas of the ten directions. In the ultimate sense, primordially, she attained the state of original wakefulness that is the very essence of the female buddha Prajñaparamita. However, to portray her background in a way that ordinary disciples can comprehend, here is her story.

Long ago, in a past eon, in the world called Myriad Lights, there was a buddha known as Drum Thunder. It was in the presence of this buddha that Tara, as the princess Wisdom Moon, first formed the resolve to attain supreme enlightenment. It was here that she took the oath to work for the welfare of all beings in the form of a woman until the whole of samsara is emptied.

In accordance with her vow, she practiced day and night, becoming able to liberate in a single day one hundred billion sentient beings from their mundane mind-state, allowing them to attain the 'acceptance of the nonarising of all things.' She was given the name Arya Tara, the Sublime Savioress, the mere recollection of whose name dispels both samsara's suffering and the shortcomings of the passive state of nirvana.

Following this, she took the vow in front of Buddha Amoghasiddhi to protect all beings of the ten directions from fear and all kinds of harm. On another occasion, she acted as an emanation of Avalokiteshvara's wisdom in order to assist him in working for the liberation of all beings. In this way, her life examples surpass the reach of ordinary thought.

Particularly in this world, during the Golden Age, the compassionate Avalokiteshvara taught one hundred million Vajrayana tantras of Tara on Mount Potala in India, and has continued up through this *Age of Strife* to teach medium and concise versions of the tantras that accord with people's capacity. These practices pacify the eight and sixteen types of fear, and cause the wish-fulfilling attainment of all needs and aims. Ultimately, through these practices one can realize the wisdom body of Mahamudra. There are innumerable wonderful stories of past practitioners to support this.

Since Arya Tara is the activity of all buddhas embodied in a single form, her blessings are swifter than those of any other deity. Most of the learned and accomplished masters of India and Tibet kept her as their main practice and attained siddhi. That is why we today have such a boundless supply of practices and instructions of Arya Tara.

The Twenty-One Taras described by Jamyang Khyentse Wangpo

The Tara practice involves the praises to the twenty-one Taras to protect against twenty-one types of harmful influences. Here is a list of the twenty manifestations of Tara based on Jamyang Khyentse Wangpo's writings.

The White Pacifying Tara: She protects from general decline in the world and beings, adversity, attack from both physical and immaterial beings, all sickness, evil influence, curses, black magic, strife, and conceptual thinking.

Bhagavati Vajra Tara who Protects Against Harm from the Earth: She protects from earthquake and avalanche in the outside world, as well as inner sickness and evil influence caused by the negative emotion pride.

The Red Tara who Protects Against Harm from Water: She protects from all harm from water in the outside world, including flooding, shipwreck, polluted drinking water, and drowning, as well as sickness and evil influence caused by the negative emotion desire.

The Tara who Protects Against Harm from Fire: She protects from harm from fire in the outside world, including wildfire and arson, as well as sickness and evil influence caused by the negative emotion of anger.

The Tara who Protects Against Harm from Wind: She protects from harm from wind in the outside world, hurricanes and storms caused by evil spirits, as well as sickness and evil influence caused by the negative emotion of jealousy.

The Yellow Tara of Enrichment: She increases all kinds of prosperity and wealth in the world, as well as intelligence and eloquence.

The Tara who Protects Against Harm from Meteors, Lightning and Hailstorms: She protects from harm caused by evil spirits or curses in the form of meteors, hailstorms, lightning, violent rainstorms, and snow damage, as well as sickness and evil influence caused by the negative emotions of desire, hatred, and envy.

The Tara who Protects Against Harm from Weapons: She protects from warfare and fighting in the outside world, persecution from an oppressor, as well as sickness and evil influence caused by the negative emotions anger and jealousy.

The Tara who Protects Against Harm from Tyrants: She protects from hostility, imprisonment and punishment by rulers, governors, and chieftains in the outside world, as well as sickness and evil influence caused by the negative emotions hatred, conceit, craving, and envy.

The Tara who Protects Against Harm from Banditry: She protects from robbery, theft, and murder by bandits, robbers or thieves in the outside world, as well as sickness and evil influence caused by the negative emotions jealousy, desire, anger and greed.

The Tara of Magnetizing: She protects from suffering by mastering external phenomena and the prana-mind within, and gives mastery over all needs and aims.

The Tara who Protects Against Harm from Spirits: She protects from the three types of evil spirits in the outside world, as well as sickness and evil influence caused by the eight classes of demons.

The Tara who Protects Against Harm from Elephants: She protects from attacks by fierce and powerful animals, elephants, horses, buffaloes, and domestic and wild animals, as well as sickness and evil influence caused by the negative emotions arrogance and ferocity.

The Tara who Protects Against Harm from Lions: She protects from attacks by lions, tigers, leopards, bears, wolves and jackals in the outside world, as well as sickness and evil influence caused by the negative emotions anger, craving, envy, and haughtiness.

The Tara who Protects Against Harm from Snakes: She protects from attacks by vipers, spiders, scorpions, rabid dogs and other kinds of poisonous creatures, as well as sickness and evil influence caused by the negative emotions dullness, ill will, covetousness, and wrong views.

The Black Subjugating Tara: She protects against all kinds of black magic, curses, spells, epidemics, and all evil forces, material as well as immaterial.

The Tara who Protects Against Harm from Disease: She pacifies sickness caused by the environment, plants, and so forth, and especially diseases caused by imbalance in the elements in the body, as well as protecting against illness, contagious disease and evil influences created by the 21,000 inner disturbances.

The Tara who Protects Against Fear of Death: She protects from direct and indirect attacks by opponents in the outside world that prevent one from maintaining a spiritual life, as well as the inner flow of deluded thinking that creates the fear of not being able to sustain oneself.

The Tara who Protects Against Fear of Poverty: She protects from decline in prosperity, economy and the ten virtuous actions in the outside world, as well as from the suffering of poverty created by miserliness, envy and craving.

The Tara who Protects Against Fear of Failure: She protects from unsuccessful endeavors in business, farming or any other project in the outside world, as well as the worry, misery, and mental pain caused by attachment and anger, competitiveness and indecision.

These were extracts from the Chokling Tersar empowerment manuals written by Jamyang Khyentse Wangpo and the fifteenth Gyalwang Karmapa.

Trulshik Adeu Rinpoche mentioned that the great Tibetan master Taranatha has written a detailed and inspiring scripture narrating the story of how Tara developed the resolve set on supreme enlightenment, the series of incarnations she went through, and how she finally awakened to the true and complete enlightenment of a buddha.

Endnotes

1 The Tibetan title is: *dgongs gter sgrol ma'i zab tig las* ༔ *legs so gsum gyi don khrid bzhugs* ༔

2 Luk, Charles, trans. 1972, *The Vimalakirti Nirdesa Sutra*, Boston: Shambhala Publications p. 78-79

3 "Her right hand, in the mudra of supreme giving, transforms into the gesture of giving refuge, below which I and all those to be protected are relieved of all fear. Since you yourself are in the form of Tara you imagine anyone who seeks protection comes under Tara's right hand, including you in your normal form. Some people then think that Tara has a very big hand, but simply imagine that those who need protection most are directly beneath while all the others are gathered around." Orgyen Tobgyal Rinpoche, unpublished teaching, 2002.

4 "Personally I am very fond of this Tara practice of *Zabtik Drölma*. Among the seven lines of transmission that Chokgyur Lingpa was endowed with, this one comes through mind treasure (*gongter*). This practice includes outer, inner and innermost sadhanas. This particular Tara practice is connected to a specific empowerment, known as a permission blessing or entrustment, written by Jamgön Kongtrül and known as *The Mandala Ritual that is The Essence of the Two Accumulations*. This *Zabtik Drölma* is very widespread and practiced by almost all the Nyingma practitioners as well as most Sakyas and Kagyüs. Oddly enough, they do not know who wrote it, as the colophon is not included with the text. The colophon was inserted after the inner and innermost sadhanas, which followed this one. Therefore, you might say, its tail accidentally got cut off. This Tara practice is endowed with incredible blessings. The present Dzongsar Khyentse Rinpoche told me that he considers this Tara practice as the most profound of all Chokgyur Lingpa's termas. In Bhutan, he personally sponsors it to be done one hundred thousand times annually." Orgyen Tobgyal Rinpoche, unpublished teaching, 2002.

5 From oral teachings of Adeu Rinpoche.

6 Tulku Urgyen Rinpoche, published in *Repeating the Words of the Buddha*.

7 Tulku Urgyen Rinpoche, *As It Is*, (Boudhanath: Rangjung Yeshe Publications, 2000) Vol. 2, p. 83.

8 Tulku Urgyen Rinpoche, *As It Is*, (Boudhanath: Rangjung Yeshe Publications, 2000) Vol. 2, p. 168.

9 Tulku Urgyen Rinpoche, *As It Is*, (Boudhanath: Rangjung Yeshe Publications, 1999) Vol. 1, p. 36.

10 Tulku Urgyen Rinpoche, unpublished teaching 1984.

11 For more details, see *Dzogchen Essentials*, (Boudhanath: Rangjung Yeshe Publications, 2004).

12 The title is: *The Essence of the Two Attainments: A clarification of The Essential Instruction on the Threefold Excellence, According to the Mind Treasure Drölma Zabtig, The Profound Essence of Tara.* (In Tibetan: *dgongs gter sgrom ma zab tig las, legs so gsum gyi don khrid gsal bar bkod pa grub gnyis thig le zhes bya ba bzhugs so.*)

13 The eight metaphors for magical illusion are listed in various ways and include: a reflection of the moon in water, optical illusion, mirage, dream, echo, castle of the *gandharvas*, hallucination, rainbow, lightning, bubbles on the surface of water, and reflection in a mirror.

14 A famous chant by Bengar Jampal Zangpo.

15 Adeu Rinpoche mentioned that, "Among Chokgyur Lingpa's termas, there is another Tara practice called *The Mandala of the Twenty-one Taras*, which is one of the four deities to dispel obstacles associated with the Barchey Künsel, which I also practice."

16 This cave is in Shelpuk, Dzomnang near Derge, eastern Tibet.

17 It is commonly known as *The Lotus Sutra* or *The Saddharma Pundarika Sutra*.

18 See Note 3.

19 Jokyab Rinpoche mentions these twenty in a footnote in the *Light of Wisdom, Vol. 1. The Sutra that Admonishes to Superior Intention* says: Maitreya, there are twenty defects of distraction. What are these twenty? Maitreya, they are not to have controlled your body, not to have controlled your speech, not to have controlled your mind, to have great desire, to have great hatred, to have great dullness, to be tainted by mundane conversation, to have completely strayed away from supramundane conversation, to associate with people who do not respect the Dharma, to have fully cast away the Dharma, to

consequently be harmed by the maras, to associate with people who
are careless, to be careless oneself, to be dominated by conception and
discernment, to completely stray away from great learning, to fail to
achieve shamatha and vipashyana, to fail quickly to maintain pure
conduct, to completely stray away from rejoicing in the Buddha, to
completely stray away from rejoicing in the Dharma, to completely
stray away from rejoicing in the Sangha. Maitreya, understand
that these twenty are the defects of taking delight in distraction. A
bodhisattva after having applied examination will take delight in
solitude and never become completely disheartened.

20 This outline follows the general system of the four tantras: Kriya
Tantra, Charya Tantra, Yoga Tantra, and Anuttara Yoga Tantra.

21 A mantra that brings to mind the emptiness of all things, either in
actuality or as a mental imitation.

22 Adeu Rinpoche explained that "sideways" means written from
Tara's front towards her back.

23 You enter the ranks of a buddha.

24 In *Light of Wisdom, Vol. 2,* Jamgön Kongtrül explains: The three
fields means that the solid clinging to your body by regarding it
as ordinary is perfected into the deity's bodily form. That is to say,
at first, that the vivid presence is perfected means that the bodily
form, attributes, ornaments, and attire of the particular deity you
have cultivated in your mental field is perceived as precisely and
distinctly as a reflection in a mirror. Next, through the power of
having trained your mind to the utmost, the mudra-form of the
deity manifests in actuality in the sense field, such as before your
eyes; not as mere imagination. Third, as signs that physical pliancy
is attained by means of the body being fully refined by mind, the
deity is manifest in the tangible bodily field. The four measures of
clarity are distinct, alive, vibrant and vivid; and the four measures
of steadiness are unmoving, unchanging, utterly unchangeable, and
yet totally flexible.

25 It is important to receive the practical details of these *tsalung*
teachings on the channels and energy-winds directly from your
teacher.

26 These teachings on the third empowerment are extremely secret
and restricted to practitioners who have received the proper
empowerments and instructions from their teacher. The student
needs to be adept in the various yoga exercises that lead up to this

and complete them before taking a consort. As intriguing and interesting as these teachings are, we are unable to openly publish them due to secrecy and our teacher's restrictions. However, we encourage sincere practitioners to connect with a lineage that has these instructions and a teacher who is willing to guide such a practitioner. Please refer to such oral instructions when requesting teachings. Interestingly enough, it is quite rare and difficult to find texts that apply specifically to the female yoga practices. Most instructions are given from the male perspective.

27 Once more, we are unable to disclose these teachings specific to inner heat practice associated with the Six Doctrines of Naropa.

PADMASAMBHAVA

CHOKGYUR LINGPA

JAMYANG KHYENTSE WANGPO

JAMGÖN KONGTRÜL, THE FIRST

Contact Addresses for Teachings and Retreats

For information regarding programs and recorded and published teachings in the lineage of Tulku Urgyen Rinpoche, please access one of the following websites:

Shedrub Development Mandala
WWW.SHEDRUB.ORG

Rangjung Yeshe Gomdé, USA
WWW.GOMDEUSA.ORG

Rangjung Yeshe Gomdé, Denmark
WWW.GOMDE.DK

Rangjung Yeshe Publications
WWW.RANGJUNG.COM